Spelling Success

CLASS 7

Peter Clutterbuck

Blake
EDUCATION
Better ways to learn

To Jessie O'Brien

Spelling Success Class 7

Published by Scholastic India Pvt. Ltd.
A-27, Ground Floor, Sigma Centre
Infocity-1, Sector 34, Gurgaon-122001 (India)
Info-in@scholastic.asia

Author: Peter Clutterbuck
Editor: Kerry Davies
Cover and internal design: Janice Bowles
Typesetter: Julian Mole, Post Pre Press.

ISBN: 978-93-5471-874-8
First edition 2010
This reprint edition: June 2024
Printed in India

Contents

Term 1

✓ Tick when completed

Term 2

✓ Tick when completed

Contents continued

About This Book

The *Successful Spelling* series provides students with learning activities that embrace the different elements of the spelling system. Each book focuses on the different scope and sequences in the development of spelling skills for each age group or skill level.

These books are not a complete spelling course in themselves, neither are they meant to be, but they provide both students and teachers with the content needed to produce best practices in spelling.

The activities in each book are sequential through the four terms of the school year. This means that it's best to start at the beginning of the Term 1 section and work though to the end, before commencing Term 2 activities, and so on. There are 76 units in this book, 18 per term plus four Review and Test units. Each term is divided into the four areas of knowledge that need to be understood and learned in order to develop a comprehensive mastery of spelling:

Phonological Knowledge — how words sound

Word Function Knowledge — how word function can change spelling

Meaning Knowledge — how context can change word form

Word History Knowledge — how words have been derived

The Phonological Knowledge and the Word Function Knowledge sections include Revision and Test sheets for each term. Four units of Review and Test sheets covering the whole book are provided at the end of Term 4.

This book also contains useful tools to support students with their spelling. At the back of the book you'll find:

- ★ Useful Words list
- ★ Some Tips for Learning to Spell
- ★ Assessment checklist
- ★ Glossary of Terms

Answers to all activities are provided in a special liftout section. A useful **topic list** for the whole year is given before the units.

Successful Spelling provides an integrated method of teaching phonics, spelling and vocabulary. These books will improve literacy skills through effective instruction and evaluation based on the latest research into how spelling is best taught and learned successfully.

Book 7 Topic Chart

Sound patterns, ai

Each word in the box contains the long **a** sound spelled as **ai**, as in **tail** and **fail**. Write the correct word in each sentence below.

quail	**available**	**quaint**	**waive**
failure	**complaint**	**slain**	**frail**
maintain	**container**	**vain**	**rainbow**
acquaint	**entertain**	**faithful**	**explain**

1. The rock band is going to __________ us during the interval.
2. The film star was an extremely arrogant and __________ person.
3. St George is said to have __________ the dragon.
4. The judge decided to __________ the fine.
5. I asked the teacher to __________ the problem again.
6. The elderly person became quite __________ after the fall.
7. We ate some roast __________ for tea.
8. It is hoped you __________ the high standard you have set.
9. His __________ to pay the fine on time cost him dearly.
10. Our teacher asked us to __________ the new student with the daily routine of our class.
11. There are lots of foreign foods __________ at this store.
12. When the attendant was rude I lodged a __________ with the manager.
13. The old cottage is really __________.
14. The water was stored in a large plastic __________.
15. After the storm the sun appeared through the clouds and formed a large __________.
16. The old dog was __________ to its master right to the end.

Write these words in sentences of your own:

fainted __________

obtain __________

aide __________

Parent/Teacher Signature　　　　Date

UNIT 2

Sound patterns, ar

The words below each contain the letters ar, pronounced as in **car** and **star**. Write the correct word in the sentences below.

cardigan	**carnival**	**departure**	**apartment**
marvellous	**charcoal**	**bargain**	**snarl**
harp	**marble**	**cargo**	**harvest**
barge	**particle**	**barter**	**guard**

1. The ________________ at the sentry post asked the visitor for identification.
2. He played the ________________ in the string section of the orchestra.
3. The dog began to ______________ when I took its bone.
4. Mike lives in an ________________ seven storeys above the street.
5. The student wore a neat woollen ________________ to the disco.
6. It was really a ________________ victory for our school team.
7. The wheat ________________ begins in early summer.
8. After the fire had died down we searched through the ________________ to find the missing keys.
9. As they usually cost $20 I got a real ________________ at only $5.
10. The ship carried vital ________________ for the isolated settlement.
11. You can often ________________ for goods at markets.
12. His ________________ last night left our team short for today's match.
13. We joined in the noisy ____________ being held in the street.
14. The statue was sculpted from white ________________.
15. The bales of wool were stacked on the ________________ ready for transport downriver.
16. A small ________________ of dust disrupted the computer program.

Write these words in sentences of your own:

marvel ____

cigar ____

bark ____

Parent/Teacher Signature Date

Sound patterns, ea

The letters **ea** can be pronounced in different ways:
(a) long **e** sound, as in **beak** (b) short **e** sound, as in **head**
(c) long **a** sound, as in **break**.

A Study the grid carefully. Find the words and write them under their sounds.

b	f	e	a	s	t	c	t
r	s	t	e	a	k	r	h
e	s	w	e	a	t	e	r
a	e	a	g	l	e	a	e
k	d	e	a	t	h	s	a
g	r	e	a	s	e	e	d

Long e sound

____

____

____

____

Short e sound

____

____

____

Long a sound

____

____

B Write each word from the box beside a word it can be linked to in some way below.

bleach	**conceal**	**measles**	**season**
weapon	**pleasant**	**thread**	**breakfast**
peach	**steak**	**dread**	**wealth**

1. mumps __________________
2. rifle __________________
3. apricot __________________
4. whiten __________________
5. sewing __________________
6. cereal __________________
7. hide __________________
8. winter __________________
9. nice __________________
10. meat __________________
11. fear __________________
12. money __________________

Parent/Teacher Signature　　　　　　　　Date

UNIT 4

Sound patterns, au and oi

A The letters **au** can be pronounced **or**, as in **sauce**, or as a short **o**, as in **sausage**.
Look at the words on the left-hand side. Write each in its correct sentence.

audition	1. The noise of the car was coming from its ________________.
authentic	2. After we ________________ the shirts we will iron them.
gauze	3. I poured the milk for the cat into the ________________.
nausea	4. We placed a ________________ over the car to protect it.
launder	5. We ate two eggs and a ________________ for lunch.
exhaust	6. The stale food gave her ________________ and vomiting.
saucer	7. The ________________ bandage was placed over the wound.
tarpaulin	8. This is an ________________ replica of an Italian sculpture.
cauliflower	9. The actors had an ________________ for the role of the star.
sausage	10. The cook shredded the ________________ to make coleslaw.

B The letters **oi** are usually pronouned as **oy**, as in **boil** and **toil**.
Write each word on the left in its correct sentence.

poise	1. We dried the ________________ from the cloth before we used it.
moisture	2. The students are not to ________________ in the street.
poisonous	3. The spaceship passed through the ________________ belt.
asteroid	4. The dress she wore was a ________________ colour.
appointment	5. It is wise to ________________ the freeway at peak hour.
rejoice	6. Do no eat this fungus as it is ________________.
avoid	7. She showed great ________________ in her dancing.
voice	8. After their victory the players began to ________________.
turquoise	9. His ________________ is quite hoarse because of the cold.
loiter	10. My ________________ with the doctor is after school.

Parent/Teacher Signature Date

Sound patterns, oo and oa

A The letters **oo** can make a long sound, as in **boot** and **pool**, or a short sound, as in **book** and **took**.
Write each word on the left in its correct sentence.

cockatoo	1. The large ________________ used its antlers to protect itself.
lagoon	2. The tall ________________ was eaten by the pandas.
schooner	3. We watched the ________________ on television.
bamboo	4. This is a ________________ table but that one is made of steel.
cartoon	5. We slept in a shady ________________ of the forest.
moose	6. Sam is ________________ bacon and eggs for breakfast.
hooded	7. The crew of the large ________________ embarked at the jetty.
wooden	8. The Aborigines hunted for mussels in the ________________.
cocoon	9. The white ________________ could say many words.
rooster	10. The bandit was ________________ when he entered the bank.
cooking	11. The ________________ stayed beside the hens.
nook	12. A green caterpillar hatched from the ________________.

B The letters **oa** are often pronounced as the long **o** sound, as in **coat** and **loaf**.
Match each **oa** word in the box with a word it can be linked to in some way.

toadstool	**loaves**	**cocoa**	**toast**	**cloak**
approach	**coast**	**loan**	**roast**	**throat**

1. meat ________________
2. bank ________________
3. ocean ________________
4. tongue ________________
5. near ________________
6. mushroom ________________
7. bread ________________
8. hot chocolate ________________
9. clothing ________________
10. breakfast ________________

Parent/Teacher Signature Date

Sound patterns, ou

The letters **ou** can be pronounced in three ways:
(a) short **u**, as in **trouble** (b) long **u**, as in **crouton**
(c) an **ow** sound, as in **loud**.

A Write each **ou** word on the left in the correct sentence.

boundary
flounder
trousers
fountain
council
scoundrel
doubtful
voucher
founder
bounty

1. The first pioneer was the ________________ of our city.
2. The boy's ________________ were torn when the dog bit him.
3. The mayor resigned as the leader of the ________________.
4. There was a ________________ for each feral animal he trapped.
5. It is ________________ we will reach the station in time.
6. I gave my friend a $10 ________________ for her birthday.
7. The mischievous boy was a real ________________.
8. A large ________________ was in the middle of the city square.
9. He caught a two-kilogram ________________ in the net.
10. The ball went over the ________________.

B The following **ou** words contain the short **u** sound or the long **u** sound. Write each beside the word it can be linked to in some way.

double	**touched**	**moustache**	**coupon**	**crouton**
cousin	**youngster**	**toucan**	**acoustics**	**cougar**

1. felt ________________
2. beard ________________
3. relation ________________
4. adult ________________
5. single ________________
6. bird ________________
7. soup ________________
8. cat ________________
9. sound ________________
10. gift ________________

Parent/Teacher Signature   Date

Revision

A Add ai, ar, ea, au or oi in the spaces.

1. ____tumn (season)
2. p____ch (fruit)
3. f____thful (loyal)
4. n____sea (sickness)
5. conc____l (hide)
6. m____sture (dampness)
7. cig____ (large tobacco product)
8. entert____n (amuse)
9. aster____d (space body)
10. ____gle (bird of prey)
11. ____de (helper)
12. c____digan (clothing)
13. s____sage (mince meat in casing)
14. m____ble (hard rock)
15. m____sles (disease)
16. p____se (control)

B Sort the ou words in the box under the headings below.

coupon	couple	double	southern	cougar	toucan
cousin	youth	routine	acoustics	trouble	touch

Short u sound		Long oo sound	
____	____	____	____
____	____	____	____
____	____	____	____

C Sort the ea words in the box under the headings below.

bleach	dread	leave	sweat	squeak	heavy
death	cheat	jealous	preach	thread	streak

Long e sound		Short e sound	
____	____	____	____
____	____	____	____
____	____	____	____

Parent/Teacher Signature Date

UNIT 8

Test 1

One word in each line is spelled incorrectly. Find the word and write it in the space.

1	He had a very pleasent walk.	1
2	The ticket will not be aivalable until next week.	2
3	It is important that you manetain your efforts.	3
4	We want to aquaint you with our friends.	4
5	The statue was carved from marbel.	5
6	The departchu time has been changed.	6
7	We got a real bargin at the sale.	7
8	I ate a bowl of cereal for brekkfast.	8
9	The chemicals are very poisinos.	9
10	The band is going to entatain us.	10
11	We smeared greese on the rusty joint.	11
12	The large eagle siezed the prey in its talons.	12
13	I placed the cup and sorcer on the table.	13
14	The workers cut down the tall thick bambu.	14
15	Mr Smith has a large, bushy mustache.	15

Total correct ______ / 15

Parent/Teacher Signature Date

Test 2

Choose the correct spelling of the word in brackets and write it in the space.

1	I am (doubtful, doubull, doutfull) that he will come.	1
2	I purchased a (voucha, vowcher, voucher) for $10.	2
3	The (cooga, cougar, couger) tracked its prey quietly.	3
4	The ball went over the (boundry, boundary, boundery).	4
5	From the (cockoon, cocune, cocoon) hatched a moth.	5
6	We cooked a (roast, rowst, roste) for lunch.	6
7	This (cokatu, cokatoo, cockatoo) can say several words.	7
8	I grew (cauliflours, colliflowers, cauliflowers) in the garden.	8
9	This chemical is (poisonous, porsinous, poisinus).	9
10	The chef cooked the (sausiges, sosages, sausages).	10
11	A rifle is a dangerous (weapon, wepun, weapin).	11
12	We have to (separate, seperate, seprate).	12
13	We all enjoyed the street (canival, carnival, carnivel).	13
14	My old dog is really (faithful, faithfull, faythful).	14
15	It is a (marvellus, marvellous, mavelis) day for the race.	15

Total correct ________
15

Parent/Teacher Signature Date

UNIT 10

Forming nouns

When you change one part of speech into another, spelling changes are always necessary. For example, if you change the noun **circle** to an adjective, you get **circular**, or to a verb, you get **circulate** or **circularise**.

Change the verb in brackets at the end of each sentence to a noun to fit the meaning.

1. The scientists made an important __________________. (discover)
2. The witness gave an accurate __________________ to the police. (describe)
3. His blatant __________________ left us all disappointed. (deceive)
4. The statue was really a wonderful __________________. (create)
5. I get an __________________ of pocket money each week. (allow)
6. When I won the trophy I had to give an __________________ speech. (accept)
7. Their __________________ in cleaning the room was helpful. (assist)
8. The __________________ he made was quite accurate. (calculate)
9. It was a serious __________________ they made against me. (accuse)
10. I am sure we have made the right __________________. (choose)
11. The victims received a lot of money in __________________. (compensate)
12. At the __________________ of the match we will leave. (complete)
13. We went to the airport to witness his final __________________. (depart)
14. A large __________________ took place in the street. (explode)
15. I have a very high __________________ of his work. (expect)
16. The __________________ of the monument was a disaster. (destroy)

Write each of these words in a sentence of your own:

explain ____

explanation ____

complete ____

completion ____

Parent/Teacher Signature Date

Forming adjectives

When you change a word into another part of speech you must make changes in spelling. To form an adjective from a noun you must add a suffix. Sometimes the base word also changes spelling (**hunger, hungry**).

Write the adjective that can be formed from the noun in the brackets at the end of each sentence. For example, from the noun **safety** you can get the adjective **safe**.

1. We were very ________________ crossing the highway. (caution)
2. The footpath is ________________ in shape. (circle)
3. Tom is extremely ________________ and tries hard all the time. (industry)
4. The goods on that table are quite ________________. (expense)
5. We sat in the ________________ lounge chair. (comfort)
6. The drought was ________________ to the farmers. (disaster)
7. That was a very ________________ prank he played on us. (humour)
8. These fungi can be quite ________________ to your health. (injury)
9. It was very ________________ he wasn't injured badly. (fortune)
10. This is really a ________________ story. (fable)
11. We booked our passage on the ________________ ocean liner. (luxury)
12. The mayor is an ________________ person in our city. (influence)
13. These toadstools are very ________________. (poison)
14. This is a ________________ jumper. (wool)
15. The team was at last ________________. (victory)
16. The small door is a ________________ shape. (triangle)

Use these words in sentences of your own:

miracle (n) ________________

miraculous (adj) ________________

star (n) ________________

starry (adj) ________________

Parent/Teacher Signature   Date

UNIT 12

Internal doubled consonants

The following words contain doubled consonants. Double consonants may occur naturally in a word (**follow**), or from what we call assimilated, or absorbed, prefixes (see glossary), as for **accumulate**.

Add a word from the box to complete the sentences below.

cappuccino	**occurred**	**accordion**	**affection**
hiccups	**tobacco**	**accountant**	**forgotten**
moccasins	**desiccated**	**corrosion**	**caffeine**
successful	**broccoli**	**traffic**	**jewellery**

1. Smoking ________________ is an unhealthy habit.
2. I had a cup of ________________ coffee at the Italian café.
3. Our team was ________________ in the finals, winning all matches.
4. An accident ________________ at the crossroads last night.
5. I bought some ________________ coconut from the supermarket.
6. There is a lot of ________________ on the freeway today.
7. Gosh! I have ________________ the name of that man already.
8. The rich lady wore expensive ________________.
9. The ________________ in the rusty pipes soon made them useless.
10. My uncle plays an ________________ in a small band.
11. My favourite vegetable is ________________.
12. I gave my mother a pair of ________________ for her feet.
13. He drank some gulps of water to try to cure his ________________.
14. My ________________ has at last completed my tax return.
15. Tammy showed ________________ towards the little kitten.
16. This coffee has a high level of ________________ in it.

Write these words in sentences of your own:

antenna ____

summit ____

hessian ____

Parent/Teacher Signature   Date

Adding the suffix ly

UNIT 13

Spelling changes are usually needed when you change a word such as an adjective into an adverb ending in **ly**.

Different words have different changes:

★ Some simply add **ly**.
Example: plain, plainly

★ If the word ends in **y** change the **y** to **i** and add **ly**.
Example: hearty, heartily

★ If the word ends in **le**, drop the **e** and add **y**. Example: noble, nobly

★ If the word ends in **ful** or **al**, simply add **ly**.
Example: skilful, skilfully

A Add **ly** to each word in the box and write it in its correct sentence below.

gentle	**lazy**	**hungry**	**probable**
sweet	**sudden**	**annual**	**true**
anxious	**easy**	**lucky**	**fatal**

1. He signed the letter Yours ____________.
2. Someone was ____________ injured in the collision.
3. ____________ no one was hurt in the accident.
4. The mother lifted the newborn baby very ____________.
5. The kangaroo ____________ jumped over the tall hedge.
6. The children's choir sang the hymns ____________.
7. Jack leaned ____________ against the wall and yawned.
8. The troops were ____________ ambushed by the enemy.
9. This fete is held ____________ each September.
10. We waited ____________ for news of the lost child.
11. The starving boy ate the food ____________.
12. It will ____________ be at least three o'clock before we get there.

B Write these in sentences of your own, making the words end in **ly**:

1. merry ____
2. patient ____

Parent/Teacher Signature   Date

UNIT 14

Revision

A Change the word in the brackets to an adjective. Make the spelling changes necessary.

1. a ______________ attack (coward)
2. an ______________ car (expense)
3. a ______________ person (fame)
4. a ______________ jumper (wool)
5. a ______________ sky (star)
6. a ______________ concert (noise)
7. a ______________ seat (comfort)
8. my ______________ food (favour)
9. a ______________ dog (faith)
10. a ______________ day (beauty)
11. an ______________ hug (affection)
12. a ______________ grave (water)

B In the spaces add the double consonants that are needed.

1. bi____abong (waterway)
2. ba____erina (dancer)
3. embe____le (steal)
4. e____ential (vital, needed)
5. ho____ible (terrible, bad)
6. je____ison (throw overboard)
7. ma____oth (extinct elephant)
8. qua____el (argument)
9. sci____ors (cutting implements)
10. vi____age (small town)
11. fe____et (small animal)
12. a____omplished (did, attained)

C Make the words in the brackets end in **ly**.

1. buying ______________ (cheap)
2. yawning ______________ (weary)
3. injured ______________ (fatal)
4. dividing ______________ (equal)
5. driving ______________ (careful)
6. wishing ______________ (hopeful)
7. playing ______________ (happy)
8. speaking ______________ (sensible)
9. sitting ______________ (comfortable)
10. waiting ______________ (anxious)
11. singing ______________ (merry)
12. playing ______________ (noisy)

Parent/Teacher Signature Date

Test

The underlined word in each sentence is spelled incorrectly. Write the correct spelling of the word on the line at the end of the sentence.

1	The departchu of the plane was ten minutes late.	1
2	She made a serious acussation against him.	2
3	Mary has given me a lot of asisstence for many years.	3
4	The mayor is a most inflewential person.	4
5	These gifts are very expinsive.	5
6	This plate is tryangular in shape.	6
7	At the footwear shop I bought a pair of mocasins.	7
8	The accident ocurred at the crossroads.	8
9	The antena of our television needs replacing.	9
10	This fete is held anualy.	10
11	I don't think it could possibley be true.	11
12	The baby was gentley lifted by the nurse.	12
13	He had a succesfull day at the carnival.	13
14	This is a most comfortible lounge.	14
15	I did not believe his explarnation.	15

Total correct ______ / 15

Parent/Teacher Signature Date

UNIT 16

Vowel alternations, short to long

When you change a word to another form of the word, sometimes the pronunciation of the vowel in the base word changes, while the base word spelling does not change. For example, the short **i** in **criminal** changes to a long **i** in **crime**.

The word in brackets at the end of each sentence has a short vowel sound. In the space write the form of the word that fits the meaning of the sentence and has a long vowel sound.
Example: pose (long **o**), position (short **o**)

1. The hot ________________ from the fire burned his fingers. (flammable)
2. Riley is a competent ________________. (athletic)
3. I ask you ________________ not to do that again. (pleasant)
4. It is time to ________________ one way or the other. (decision)
5. I can only ________________ he did not know. (assumption)
6. This company can ________________ thousands of cars. (production)
7. We fled when the ________________ began to erupt. (volcanic)
8. That was a ________________ thing to do for the prisoners. (humanity)
9. We hid in the ________________ during the storm. (cavity)
10. It is time for us to ________________ our system again. (revision)
11. The dry wood will ________________ when we light it. (ignition)
12. Our teacher is a very ________________ person. (wisdom)
13. We will ________________ the cake equally. (division)
14. The doctor made a ________________ decision about the patient. (gravity)
15. The work is second ________________ to the old hand. (natural)
16. The next ________________ of the show is on tonight. (episodic)

Use these words in sentences of your own:

convene ____

convention ____

serene ____

serenity ____

Parent/Teacher Signature   Date

Long vowel sound to schwa

The vowel sound that often occurs in an unstressed syllable, such as the **uh** sound in the first syllable of the word **above** and the **er** sound in the last syllable of **major**, is called schwa. When you change the form of a word, a stressed syllable with a long vowel sound often becomes the short schwa sound.

Change the words with a long vowel sound in the brackets to one with a short schwa sound that fits the meaning of the sentence.

1. The ________________ of people voted for the change. (major)
2. A ________________ scene was staged for Christmas. (native)
3. You need much ________________ before the event. (prepare)
4. Tom is a distant ________________ of mine. (relate)
5. The athletes enjoyed the strong ________________. (compete)
6. She could not remember the ________________ of the bank safe. (combine)
7. She gave a clear ________________ of the word. (define)
8. There is a big ________________ between the wealthy and the poor in this country. (divide)
9. The new girl possesses a lot of ________________ in sport. (able)
10. We accepted her kind ________________. (invite)
11. Michelle is now a permanent ________________ of our town. (reside)
12. The ________________ of this mixture is not known. (compose)
13. The criminal was taken into ________________. (custodian)
14. The newly designed building has good ________________. (stable)
15. The statue was moved to a new ________________. (pose)
16. She gave a faultless ________________ of the poem. (recite)

Use these words in sentences of your own:

social ________________________________

society ________________________________

famous ________________________________

infamous ________________________________

Parent/Teacher Signature Date

UNIT 18

Latin root words

Many of the everyday words we use have come from Latin, the language spoken by the ancient Romans. For example, from the Latin root word for water, **aqua**, we get words like **aquatic**, **aquarium** and **aquamarine**.

Write a word in the space that has been formed from the Latin root named below.

1. The ______________ of the jet is 20,000 metres. (altus = high)
2. Some cars are automatic but many have a ______________ gear change. (manus = hand)
3. The doctor had to attend to an ______________. (mergo = I plunge)
4. The ______________ carried a nuclear warhead. (mitto = I send)
5. The surgeon performed the heart ______________. (opus = work)
6. The ______________ was hit by the speeding car. (pedis = foot)
7. My brother has begun ______________ school. (primus = first)
8. The wealthy man owns a lot of ______________ in the city. (proprius = one's own)
9. They celebrated their fiftieth ______________. (annus = year)
10. I hope the principal's address will be ______________. (brevis = short)
11. The doctors conducted a post-mortem on the ______________. (corpus = body)
12. The strong ______________ swept the swimmers away. (curro = I run)
13. The ______________ applauded the choir loudly. (audio = I hear)
14. James has been elected ______________ of the team. (caput = head)
15. After he left the army Will became a ______________ once again. (civis = citizen)
16. Sally was ______________ of her school. (duco = I lead)

Write a word we use that would come from each of these Latin root words:

pedis = foot ______________ dens = tooth ______________

numerus = number ______________

Parent/Teacher Signature Date

Sound patterns, ei and ie

A The letters **ei** can be pronounced as a long **e** sound, as in **deceit** and **either**, or as a long **a** sound, as in **weight** and **eight**. Write each word on the left in its correct sentence.

receipt	1. We painted the ________________ of the room white.
seize	2. I am sure ________________ Sam or Joe did it.
deceived	3. The eagle tried to ________________ the animal in its talons.
ceiling	4. The shopkeeper gave me a tax ________________ for the goods.
conceited	5. We were sure ________________ Mary nor Sue stole the money.
either	6. The cunning thief easily ________________ the elderly man.
neither	7. The film star is both arrogant and ________________.
weight	8. Our next door ________________ comes from Vietnam.
vein	9. The children had fun riding the snow in their ________________.
freight	10. The doctor removed a ________________ from the man's leg.
neighbour	11. The ________________ of the bag dragged him under the water.
sleigh	12. This ship carried ________________ to Tasmania.

B The letters **ie** can be pronounced as a long **e** sound, as in **piece**, or as a long **i** sound, as in **pie**.
The words in the box have either the long **e** sound or the long **i** sound. Write each in its correct sentence below.

thieves	**handkerchief**	**believe**	**achievement**	**replied**
pierced	**shield**	**relieved**	**applied**	**relied**

1. We were ________________ when they told us he was well.
2. I did not ________________ his incredible story.
3. The horns of the bull ________________ the man's chest.
4. The ________________ hid the jewels in the cellar.
5. It was a great ________________ for someone so young to get the position.
6. She wiped her nose with a ________________.
7. Mike ________________ for the job as baker at the new factory.
8. The children ________________ that they would all help clean up.
9. We ________________ on her skills to guide us home.
10. The knight had his coat of arms displayed on his ________________.

Parent/Teacher Signature Date

UNIT 20

Sound patterns, ee

The letters **ee** are pronounced as a long **e** sound, as in **fleet** and **street**.
Each word in the box contains the long **e** sound. Write each word in the correct space below.

guarantee	**steeple**	**cheerful**	**exceed**
corroboree	**eerie**	**breeze**	**volunteer**
succeed	**canteen**	**teenager**	**auctioneer**
sneeze	**committee**	**squeeze**	**coffee**

1. The pollen of the flowers made him ________________ loudly.
2. Michelle is twelve years old but on her next birthday she will become a ________________.
3. We bought some sandwiches at the factory ________________.
4. The ________________ called for higher bids from the buyers.
5. I always drink a cup of hot ________________ for breakfast.
6. It is unwise to ________________ the speed limit on this stretch of road.
7. Our teacher is very ________________ today because it is the last day of school.
8. A light ________________ helped the yachts reach the lighthouse.
9. An Aboriginal ________________ was held to educate the tourists.
10. Although he failed last week he is sure to ________________ this time.
11. This new motor has a ________________ of ten years.
12. The tall ________________ of the church is under repair.
13. An ________________ noise came from the deserted home.
14. Our football club has a ten-member ________________.
15. The large python began to ________________ its prey before eating it.
16. I decided to ________________ to raise money for a charity.

Write these words in sentences of your own:

degree ________________________________

toffee ________________________________

screech ________________________________

Parent/Teacher Signature　　　　　　　　Date

Sound patterns, er

The letters **er** are usually pronounced as they look, as in **fern** and **stern**.

A Write each word containing the **er** sound from the box beside a word it can be linked to in some way below. Note that some words in the box use the schwa **er** vowel sound that occurs in an unstressed syllable.

verse	**feather**	**camera**	**liberty**
poverty	**battery**	**desert**	**permanent**
stationery	**passenger**	**boomerang**	**mystery**
lantern	**northern**	**answer**	**weather**

1. photograph ____________________
2. cactus ____________________
3. train ____________________
4. novel ____________________
5. poem ____________________
6. torch ____________________
7. question ____________________
8. wealth ____________________
9. climate ____________________
10. captivity ____________________
11. electricity ____________________
12. temporary ____________________
13. envelopes ____________________
14. Aboriginal ____________________
15. southern ____________________
16. bird ____________________

B Write each **er** word in the space beside its correct meaning.

leather	1.	____________________	sure
persuade	2.	____________________	treated hide of animals
modern	3.	____________________	large African animal
altered	4.	____________________	a meal course
interrupt	5.	____________________	where young plants are raised
machinery	6.	____________________	to butt in to a conversation
certain	7.	____________________	changed, made different
rhinoceros	8.	____________________	up to date
dessert	9.	____________________	tools, implements for working
nursery	10.	____________________	to sway someone's thinking

Parent/Teacher Signature Date

UNIT 22

Sound patterns, or

The sound unit **or** can have different spellings. Here are four of them: (a) **or**, as in **cord** (b) **oor**, as in **door** (c) **oar**, as in **soar** (d) **au**, as in **audible**.

A Write each **or** word in its correct sentence (some of the words use the schwa vowel sound, where the **or** is in an unstressed syllable).

mirror
gorgeous
enormous
gorilla
orchestra
dormitory
organise
shortage
portrait
tortoise

1. We saw a ________________ in the rainforests of Africa.
2. Our teacher hopes to ________________ an excursion for us soon.
3. The ________________ played many of our favourite tunes.
4. The famous ________________ was hung at the art gallery.
5. The ________________ was kept in the local aquarium.
6. An ________________ elephant lumbered across the street.
7. The boy gazed in the ________________ to tidy his hair.
8. The school boarders were housed in a large ________________.
9. The baby girl looked quite ________________ in her pretty dress.
10. There will be a ________________ of grain if this drought continues.

B Match each **or** word in the box to a word below that it can be linked to in some way.

orchard	**torment**	**anchor**	**portion**	**orphan**
cord	**mirror**	**tractor**	**encore**	**author**

1. book ________________
2. image ________________
3. parent ________________
4. fruit ________________
5. rope ________________
6. whole ________________
7. performance ________________
8. farm ________________
9. ship ________________
10. tease ________________

Write these **or** words in sentences of your own:

normal ________________________________

tornado ________________________________

Parent/Teacher Signature Date

Sound patterns, ur and ow

A The letters ur can be pronounced as an er sound, as in **burn** and **church**.
These words each contain ur but they have been cramped up. Write each beside its correct meaning below.

surgeonturkeysuburbturnipburgerpurposepurpleturtleblurrybur-den

1. root vegetable ____________
2. farmyard bird ____________
3. takeaway food ____________
4. colour ____________
5. load ____________
6. doctor who operates ____________
7. outskirts of a city ____________
8. reason, use ____________
9. hard-shelled creature ____________
10. difficult to see clearly ____________

B The letters ow can be pronounced as a long ou sound, as in **cow**, or a long o sound, as in **know**.
Find the ow words in the grid and write them under the correct heading.

d	r	o	w	s	y	l	t
b	b	l	o	w	n	o	r
u	k	n	o	w	n	w	o
r	f	u	r	r	o	w	w
r	p	o	w	d	e	r	e
o	c	o	w	a	r	d	l
w	r	a	i	n	b	o	w
t	o	w	n	s	h	i	p

ow, as in cow

____

____

____

____

____

ow, as in know

____

____

____

____

____

____

Choose any three of the words above and write them in a sentence.

1. ____________
2. ____________
3. ____________

Parent/Teacher Signature Date

UNIT 24

Sound patterns, ch

The letters **ch** can represent three sounds:
(a) **ch**, as in **chop** (b) **k**, as in **chaos** (c) **sh**, as in **chef**.

Write the words in the box in the correct sentences below.

chlorine	**parachute**	**chef**	**quiche**
chemist	**anchor**	**champagne**	**champion**
chassis	**charity**	**chemical**	**chasm**
machine	**cheque**	**chapel**	**orchestra**

1. The pilot jumped from the diving plane and opened his ________________.
2. The ship dropped ________________ in the harbour.
3. The ________________ is going to cook a surprise for us all tonight.
4. Josh became the school athletic ________________.
5. The chemical ________________ was poured into the swimming pool.
6. We bought some tablets from the ________________ in High Street.
7. I received a bank ________________ for $50.
8. The young couple were married in the ________________.
9. The wealthy lady donated a huge sum of money to a ________________.
10. At the wedding we toasted the bride and groom with ________________.
11. A deep ________________ opened in the road after the earthquake.
12. The ________________ played many of my favourite tunes.
13. The ________________ of the car needed welding repairs.
14. This ________________ is a kind of lathe for turning metal.
15. Wash your hands if you touch this ________________ as it is toxic.
16. My sister cooked us a delicious ________________ for tea.

Write these words in sentences of your own:

chess ________________________________

school ________________________________

charade ________________________________

Parent/Teacher Signature Date

Revision

A Write the words in the box under the headings below.

chemist	**champagne**	**machine**	**charade**
chassis	**chlorine**	**charity**	**cholera**
charcoal	**chillblain**	**chronic**	**chocolate**

ch sound as in chisel	**k sound as in school**	**sh sound as in chef**
______	______	______
______	______	______
______	______	______
______	______	______

B Add the sound units **or**, **er** or **ee** in the spaces to complete each word.

1. br____ze (light wind)
2. passeng____ (traveller in a vehicle)
3. g____illa (large ape)
4. auction____r (salesperson)
5. auth____ (writer)
6. cam____ra (for taking photos)
7. sn____ze (involuntary cough)
8. p____trait (painting)
9. lib____ty (freedom)
10. st____ple (part of a church)
11. en____mous (huge)
12. answ____ (opposite to question)

C Sort the **ei** words in the box under the headings below.

weight	**deceive**	**receipt**	**neighbour**
conceit	**eighty**	**reign**	**seize**

Long e sound		**Long a sound**	
______	______	______	______
______	______	______	______

Parent/Teacher Signature Date

UNIT 26

Test 1

The spelling mistake in each sentence has been underlined. Write the correct spelling for the underlined word in the box.

	Sentence	
1	The shopkeeper gave me a receit for the goods.	1
2	I wiped my nose with a hankercheef.	2
3	We painted the seiling of the room white.	3
4	You must sqeeze the oranges to get the juice.	4
5	I hope you suckeed this time.	5
6	I will garantee that this will work.	6
7	The bird lost a fetha when I grabbed it.	7
8	Please do not interupt when I am speaking.	8
9	The oarkestra played many popular tunes.	9
10	The famous artist painted a poortrate of the man.	10
11	I live in a busy suberb of Melbourne.	11
12	I ate a hamberger for lunch.	12
13	I cashed the check at the bank.	13
14	These kemicals are quite poisonous.	14
15	The shassis of the car is in need of repair.	15

Total correct ______
15

Parent/Teacher Signature

Date

Test 2

For each sentence choose the correct spelling from the words in the brackets.

1. I bought the pills at the (kemist, chemist, chemest). [ ] 1
2. The ship began to (anchor, ankor, anker). [ ] 2
3. Do you know what its (perpus, purpus, purpose) is? [ ] 3
4. The children slept in a (doormitory, dormitory, dormitery). [ ] 4
5. The (tortus, tortise, tortoise) looked for food in the water. [ ] 5
6. I saw my image in the (mirra, mirror, miror). [ ] 6
7. The (orther, autha, author) of the book is my uncle. [ ] 7
8. Some countries suffer a lot of (poverty, povarty, poffarty). [ ] 8
9. We heard an (erie, eery, eerie) noise last night. [ ] 9
10. He works as an (ouctioneer, auctionier, auctioneer). [ ] 10
11. She is extremely (conceited, conceeted, connceeted). [ ] 11
12. Our (neybor, neighba, neighbour) comes from Italy. [ ] 12
13. A (vane, vein, vien) in her leg became blocked. [ ] 13
14. This is a great (achievement, acheivement, achievment). [ ] 14
15. She is a member of a (comittee, committee, committie). [ ] 15

Total correct ________ / 15

Parent/Teacher Signature   Date

Plurals, adding s or es

Nouns have two forms – singular (one) and plural (more than one).
Most nouns simply add **s** to make their plural.
Example: one table, several tables
For nouns that end in the sounds **s**, **sh**, **ch**, **z** and **x**, you add **es**. Example: one church, two churches

A Change the word in brackets to a plural and write it in the space.

1. There have been several ________________ on the highway. (crash)
2. I put the two ________________ in the car. (brush)
3. This girl has a lot of ________________ to choose from. (dress)
4. All of the ________________ are in the carpark. (bus)
5. The surgeon sewed twenty ________________ to join the severed limb. (stitch)
6. Please stack all those ________________ on the table. (box)
7. A gathering of a lot of ________________ is called a coven. (witch)
8. After the accident she needed ________________ to walk. (crutch)
9. I gave him three ________________ but he could not solve the problem. (guess)
10. Oxygen and nitrogen are two important ________________. (gas)
11. The ________________ have hidden their cubs in the lair. (fox)
12. This house has two ________________. (garage)
13. The cowboy fired two ________________ from his gun. (bullet)
14. I was hoping I did not have to wash all the ________________. (dish)
15. My three ________________ visit me frequently. (niece)

B Complete the following by changing the word to plural.

1. one egg, six ________________
2. one gash, several ________________
3. one match, lots of ________________
4. one peach, three ________________
5. one banana, two ________________
6. one arch, three ________________
7. one beach, two ________________
8. one class, several ________________

Parent/Teacher Signature Date

Plurals, words ending in y

Nouns that end in y form their plurals in two ways:

★ If there is a vowel before the final y, simply add s. Examples: one boy, two boys; one day, seven days

★ If there is a consonant before the final y, change the y to i and then add es. Example: one ferry, a fleet of ferries

A Make the word in brackets plural and write it in the space.

1. There were six ________________ in the tree. (monkey)
2. There are lots of ________________ in the jar. (lolly)
3. The new ________________ have arrived from the printer. (diary)
4. The ________________ are full of dark clouds. (sky)
5. The two large ________________ met at the bottom of the hill. (army)
6. There are lots of ________________ on the meat. (fly)
7. There are four supermarket ________________ in the yard. (trolley)
8. Both of the man's ________________ are bruised. (kidney)
9. This building is seven ________________ high. (storey)
10. There are four small ________________ in our town. (library)
11. The six ________________ formed a ring around the mushroom. (fairy)
12. Our teacher has a lot of ________________ to fulfill each day. (duty)
13. We searched both ________________ but could not find him. (alley)
14. He has made several overseas ________________ this year. (journey)
15. The horse farm has several ________________. (pony)

B Find the words in the grid and write their plural forms on the line.

p	o	p	p	y	d	i
c	t	r	a	y	o	n
i	n	a	v	y	n	j
t	l	a	d	y	k	u
y	b	o	d	y	e	r
l	o	r	r	y	y	y
l	a	u	n	d	r	y

1. ________________
2. ________________
3. ________________
4. ________________
5. ________________
6. ________________
7. ________________
8. ________________
9. ________________
10. ________________

Parent/Teacher Signature Date

UNIT 30

Plurals, words ending in o, f or fe

Most nouns that end in **o** add **es** to form their plural . However, some words, especially foreign words, simply add **s**. Examples: one hero, two heroes; one folio, several folios Some nouns ending in **f** or **fe** simply add **s** to make their plural. But some change the **f** to **v** then add **es**. Examples: one waif, two waifs; one elf, two elves

A Change the word in brackets to plural and write it in the space.

1. There are many dangerous ________________ along the coast. (reef)
2. The orange ________________ were given to the players. (scarf)
3. Oliver's job was to sharpen the three ________________. (knife)
4. We stacked the canned food on the two ________________. (shelf)
5. The six hungry ________________ chased the deer. (wolf)
6. There are several ________________ in this area. (volcano)
7. We sliced up the four ________________ to make the salad. (potato)
8. We took lots of ________________ at the picnic. (photo)
9. We could hear the ________________ across the mountain. (echo)
10. The swarms of ________________ were a pest on the picnic. (mosquito)
11. There are seven ________________ in this home. (piano)
12. The fifty stampeding ________________ did a lot of damage. (buffalo)
13. The baker has seven ________________ of bread to give away. (loaf)
14. The ten cows and their ten ________________ are in the paddock. (calf)
15. The ________________ of the houses were blown off in the storm. (roof)

B Complete the following by changing the word to plural.

1. one leaf, several ________________
2. one thief, two ________________
3. one wife, five ________________
4. one carafe, two ________________
5. one giraffe, six ________________
6. one radio, two ________________
7. one potato, nine ________________
8. one tornado, several ________________

Parent/Teacher Signature Date

Possessives

Many years ago when a student wished to show others a book belonged to her she would write Sally Thompson, her book. Today Sally would write Sally Thomson's book. The apostrophe shows that the word **her** is omitted.

To show that something is owned, always remember the following:

★ For singular nouns, add s. Don't change or leave out any letters of the original word no matter how it is spelled. Examples: boy's bike, woman's bag

★ For plural nouns not ending in s, add the apostrophe and an s ('s). Do not change the spelling of the original word. Examples: men's boots, women's shoes

★ To spell the possessive of plural nouns that end in s, add only an apostrophe. Examples: trees' leaves, boxes' contents, girls' bikes

★ For singular nouns ending in ss, add 's. Example: the boss's car

★ In compound words, add the apostrophe to the last word. Example: son-in-law's house.

★ To spell the possessive of one-syllable proper nouns that end in s, add 's. Example: the Jones's house

★ When there are several owners of one thing, only the last mentioned owner gets an apostrophe. Example: Bill and Susan's dog

A Rewrite each phrase using the correct possessive of the underlined word. The first one has been done for you.

1. the book of the girl — the *girl's book*
2. the stripes of the tigers — the ____________
3. the wings of the fairy — the ____________
4. the toys of the child — the ____________
5. the toys of the children — the ____________
6. the nest of the dove — the ____________

B Write the possessive form of each of these words.

1. babies	5. foxes	9. cousin	13. teacher
2. eagle	6. sailors	10. lions	14. dog
3. donkeys	7. student	11. daughter-in-law	15. tables
4. window	8. wolves	12. city	16. men

Parent/Teacher Signature   Date

UNIT 32

Revision

Change the words into plurals and write each in the correct sentence below.

guess	beach	potato	donkey
fly	brush	trolley	poppy
bird	thief	calf	knife
alley	garage	fox	piano

1. We counted over one hundred ________________ in the aviary.
2. Although he had ten ________________ he still couldn't get the answer.
3. There are lots of golden ________________ in Australia.
4. There are three ________________ in our town.
5. We stored the hair ________________ in the drawer.
6. Two ________________ were on the beach to take people on rides.
7. The supermarket is trying to find the six missing ________________.
8. The hunter shot five ________________.
9. We tried to keep the swarms of ________________ off the meat.
10. Our city has lots of dark, concrete ________________.
11. We picked red ________________ that were growing in the field.
12. The six ________________ were placed on the table.
13. I am going to cut six ________________ into chips.
14. Lots of ________________ were with the cows in the paddock.
15. Our school has two ________________.
16. The two ________________ were soon caught by the police.

Write these words in sentences of your own:

buffalo ________________________________

echo ________________________________

city ________________________________

Parent/Teacher Signature Date

Test

The underlined word in each sentence is incorrectly spelled. Write the word correctly in the space.

1	We ate all the five <u>tomatos</u> for lunch.	1
2	Along this coast there are many dangerous <u>reeves</u>.	2
3	There were thousands of <u>mosquitos</u> in the swamp.	3
4	There are several newborn <u>babys</u> in the hospital.	4
5	We had to wash all the different <u>dishs</u>.	5
6	Our grade was given thirty <u>diarys</u>.	6
7	Captain James Cook made several <u>journies</u>.	7
8	There are lots of <u>monkies</u> in the zoo.	8
9	Sydney and Melbourne are large <u>citys</u>.	9
10	We caught lots of <u>blowflys</u> in the trap.	10
11	Alex has suffered many <u>injurys</u> on the playing field.	11
12	She can only move with the help of two <u>crutchs</u>.	12
13	This room has several <u>mirrers</u> to look into.	13
14	We stacked the six <u>boxs</u> on the table.	14
15	I took lots of <u>photoes</u> at the reunion.	15

Total correct ______ / 15

Parent/Teacher Signature Date

UNIT 34

Compound words

Compound words are made up of two or more smaller words. Example: ham + burger = hamburger

Use a word from the box to complete each compound word below.

burger	**board**	**meal**	**sick**
glasses	**house**	**wear**	**writer**
stick	**coat**	**drum**	**paper**
break	**fever**	**truck**	**ring**

1. Mike Smith works as a sign__________.
2. She ate a bowl of oat__________ for breakfast.
3. The loud noise burst his left ear__________.
4. I ate a cheese____________ for lunch.
5. This beautiful ear__________ is made of gold.
6. We are going to depart at day__________.
7. Jack's parents bought him a new skate__________.
8. I suffer from hay__________ during spring.
9. We pasted the wall__________ on with glue.
10. After playing in the muddy pool his under__________ needed washing.
11. The police met at the court__________.
12. After the accident a tow__________ carted away one of the vehicles.
13. As it was cold he decided to wear an over__________.
14. The film star wore sun__________ to the premiere.
15. She applied some lip__________ before going out.
16. The foreign student soon became home__________.

Write these words in sentences of your own:

eyelid ______________________________

fireproof ______________________________

cookbook ______________________________

Parent/Teacher Signature Date

Elements of meaning

Words that share the same element of meaning are usually spelled with the same pattern.

Look at the words in the brackets and then write each in its correct sentence. Example: crime, criminal, criminology

1. (please, pleasant, pleasure)

a. I got a lot of __________ from his performance.

b. This student likes to __________ her teachers.

c. We had a __________ trip to the bushland.

2. (equal, equalled, equality)

a. I tried hard to __________ his performance.

b. Our country aims for all people to have __________.

c. This motor has been copied but never __________.

3. (courage, encourage, courageous)

a. Our teacher likes to __________ us to improve.

b. She won because of her __________ performance.

c. It took a lot of __________ for the person to own up.

4. (love, loving, lovable)

a. Small kittens are soft and __________.

b. The child gave his parents a __________ kiss goodbye.

c. It is said the two have fallen in __________.

5. (circle, circulation, circular)

a. She drew a __________ in her book.

b. The house is a __________ shape.

c. The medical officer checked the __________ of blood in his body.

6. (fool, fooling, foolish)

a. Don't take him seriously as he is only __________ us.

b. His __________ act damaged the walls.

c. We all thought he was just a simple __________.

Parent/Teacher Signature Date

UNIT 36

Greek root words

Many common words we use came to English through the language spoken by the ancient Greek people. For example, from the ancient Greek word **aster**, meaning star, we get words like **asterisk**, **astronomy**, **astrologer** and **disaster**.

Complete the sentences below by forming a word from the Greek root word in the brackets.

1. A terrible ________________ of the disease killed many people. (demos = people)
2. This machine is powered by ________________. (elektron = amber)
3. In language we learn about spelling and ________________. (gramma = word)
4. We had a lot of ________________ for the classmate who had lost her parents. (pathos = feeling)
5. The officer took a ________________ of the prisoner with his camera. (photos = light)
6. We measured the ________________ of the square. (metron = measure)
7. The lady took the lipstick from her ________________ bag. (kosmos = beauty)
8. She decided to study ________________ at university. (aster = a star)
9. She made an appointment with an ________________ to have her eyes checked. (optikos = sight)
10. I asked the film star for her ________________. (grapho = I write)
11. The author wrote a ________________ of the actor's life. (bios = life)
12. We received the ________________ listing all the goods for sale. (logos = word)
13. We all enjoyed playing ________________ last night. (monos = alone)
14. Australia is said to be a ________________ country. (demos = people)
15. Melbourne is a large ________________ in Victoria. (polis = city)
16. The doctor listened to my heartbeat with a ________________. (stethos = breast)

Parent/Teacher Signature Date

Sound patterns, y

The letter **y** can be pronounced as a long **e** sound, as in **pretty** and **lily**.

Use a word from the box to complete each sentence below.

poultry	**guilty**	**library**	**slippery**
mystery	**nursery**	**quality**	**finally**
happy	**luckily**	**industry**	**laundry**
battery	**securely**	**primary**	**boundary**

1. The ________________ that powered the lights in the car became flat.
2. The manager locked the goods ________________ in the vault.
3. The prisoner was found ________________ of theft.
4. Fowls, ducks and geese are known as ________________.
5. We borrowed the books from our local municipal ________________.
6. Michelle will begin her ________________ schooling next year.
7. A snake-like ________________ fish is an eel.
8. We washed the clothes in the local ________________.
9. What happened to the ship all those years ago still remains a ________________.
10. The boy was ________________ with his results.
11. The explosion wrecked the house but ________________ no one was home.
12. The ________________ of these goods seems to be improving.
13. The young trees were purchased from the ________________.
14. Although they were late they ________________ arrived.
15. The ball was kicked out over the ________________ of the field.
16. The car-making ________________ employs thousands of people.

Use these words in sentences of your own:

quantity ________________________________

extremely ________________________________

secondary ________________________________

Parent/Teacher Signature   Date

UNIT 38

Sound patterns, ar, or and er

The word endings **ar**, **or** and **er** are often sounded as unaccented syllables, as in **cellar**, **visor** and **feather**. These are Schwa vowel sounds.

A Add ar, or or er to complete each word.

1.	looking glass	mirr______	9.	kind of cheese	chedd______
2.	dish for a cup	sauc______	10.	part of volcano	crat______
3.	computer part	curs______	11.	kitchen tool	blend______
4.	baseball player	pitch______	12.	wild cat	coug______
5.	tooth	mol______	13.	farm machine	tract______
6.	thief	burgl______	14.	to do with the moon	lun______
7.	heavenly body	mete______	15.	fine sediment	powd______
8.	cutting implement	raz______	16.	disease	canc______

B Add ar, or or er to complete each word.

1. The propell______ on the old plane was made of wood.
2. The person over there is a foreign______.
3. We put the fish in the refrigerat______ .
4. She fired her revolv______ at the burglar.
5. The ship dropped anch______ in the harbour.
6. The slaught______ of the animals must have happened yesterday.
7. She is very particul______ about who she befriends.
8. The baromet______ on the wall measures atmospheric pressure.
9. She listened to the news on her transist______ radio.
10. The bank tell______ hand me the money.
11. The shape of the yard is circul______.
12. He is the auth______ of many popular books.

Parent/Teacher Signature Date

Sound patterns, ph

The letters **ph** are pronounced as an **f** sound, as in **hyphen** and **aphid**.

Study the words in the box carefully. All contain the letters ph sounded as f. Write each word beside its meaning below.

physician	**pheasant**	**elephant**	**aphids**
phobia	**pharmacy**	**hyphen**	**trophy**
telephone	**pharaoh**	**nephew**	**cipher**
alphabet	**photocopy**	**dolphin**	**sphere**

1. the letters of a language ____________
2. a chemist's shop ____________
3. a punctuation mark ____________
4. small plant-sucking insects ____________
5. a sea mammal ____________
6. a doctor or medical practitioner ____________
7. a game bird ____________
8. a fear ____________
9. large mammal with a trunk ____________
10. a prize or award ____________
11. a code ____________
12. a relation ____________
13. a ball shape ____________
14. a means of communication ____________
15. a copy of a document ____________
16. an Egyptian king ____________

Write these words in sentences of your own:

physical ____________

graph ____________

phantom ____________

Parent/Teacher Signature Date

UNIT 40

Sound patterns, qu and gh

A The letters **qu** can represent two sounds:
(a) the **kw** sound, as in **queer** (b) the **k** sound, as in **quiche**.
These **qu** words have been jammed up. Find each one and write it beside its meaning below.

quadranglequartzquaverquincequintetquiverquotientqueuequantityquag-mire

1. group of five singers ________________
2. hard yellow fruit ________________
3. container for arrows ________________
4. four-sided figure ________________
5. hard rock ________________
6. line of people ________________
7. amount ________________
8. musical note ________________
9. muddy, boggy area ________________
10. answer to a division sum ________________

B The letters **gh** at the end of a word are pronounced as an **f** sound, as in **rough**, or are silent, as in **though**.
Find all the words in the grid. Write them in the spaces.

l	a	u	g	h	t
r	o	u	g	h	h
n	e	i	g	h	r
t	h	i	g	h	o
b	o	u	g	h	u
c	o	u	g	h	g
t	o	u	g	h	h

1. Lachlan has a very deep ________________.
2. The ________________ of the tree broke in the strong wind.
3. This meat is very ________________ to chew.
4. The noise of the horse is a ________________.
5. One paper is smooth but the other is ________________.
6. The comedian made us ________________.
7. During the match he bruised his ________________.
8. We ran ________________ the corridor into the yard.

Put a tick beside those words in which the **gh** sound is **f**.
Put a cross beside those words in which the **gh** is silent.

Parent/Teacher Signature Date

Hard and soft c

The letter **c** is pronounced as a hard sound, as in **cat**, or a soft sound, as in **city**.

A Each word in the box begins with a hard **c** sound.
Write the correct word to complete the sentences below.

carpet	**curtains**	**cuckoo**	**cucumber**	**command**
carnivorous	**canvas**	**catalogue**	**continents**	**confectionery**

1. The ________________ laid its egg in the wren's nest.
2. The sails on the yacht were made of ________________.
3. Lions and tigers are ________________ animals but zebras are herbivorous.
4. We sliced the ________________ to put in the salad.
5. The general gave the ________________ to attack immediately.
6. Asia is the largest of all the ________________.
7. The new home has a thick ________________ on the lounge room floor.
8. I pulled the ________________ together to stop people peering into my room.
9. I ordered the shirt and jumper from the clothing ________________.
10. Health experts believe we eat too much ________________ today.

B Each word in the grid begins with the soft **c** sound. Find the words and write them beside their meanings.

c	i	d	e	r	c	c
c	c	c	c	c	y	e
i	e	e	e	e	c	r
r	n	l	r	l	l	t
c	s	e	e	l	o	a
l	u	r	a	a	n	i
e	s	y	l	r	e	n

1. breakfast food ________________
2. strong destructive wind ________________
3. round shape ________________
4. apple drink ________________
5. counting of the population ________________
6. sure ________________
7. underground room ________________
8. green vegetable ________________

Write these words in sentences of your own:

carnation ________________________________

cemetery ________________________________

Parent/Teacher Signature Date

UNIT 42

Hard and soft g

The letter g can be pronounced as a hard sound, as in **goat**, or a soft sound, as in **giraffe**.

Half the words in the box begin with a hard g sound while the other half begin with the soft g sound. Write each beside their meaning below.

gadget	**gladiator**	**genius**	**gymnasium**
guitar	**glacier**	**geology**	**generator**
gorilla	**guilty**	**geometry**	**generous**
galaxy	**garbage**	**germinate**	**genuine**

Hard g

1. stringed instrument ____________
2. large river of ice ____________
3. rubbish ____________
4. large ape ____________
5. small device ____________
6. large group of stars ____________
7. fighter in ancient Rome ____________
8. opposite of innocent ____________

Soft g

1. form of mathematics ____________
2. real, true ____________
3. extremely clever person ____________
4. large room for physical exercise ____________
5. very kind ____________
6. to emerge from a seed ____________
7. machine that produces electricity ____________
8. study of rocks and the Earth's surface ____________

Write these words in sentences of your own:

glutton ______________________________

gentle ______________________________

Parent/Teacher Signature Date

Revision

A Read the words in the box and then write each under its heading below.

comet	cemetery	control	genie
gallop	ginger	circus	gallant
gesture	gossip	gypsy	circuit
centipede	coffee	gallery	coconut

Hard g	Soft g	Hard c	Soft c
______	______	______	______
______	______	______	______
______	______	______	______
______	______	______	______

B Add ar, or or er to complete each word.

1. mol____ tooth
2. plumb____ mends taps and pipes
3. edit____ newspaper worker
4. circul____ round in shape
5. visit____ guest
6. sauc____ dish for a cup
7. burgl____ thief
8. freez____ object to preserve food
9. tut____ teacher
10. litt____ rubbish
11. don____ person who donates
12. schol____ student, learner

C Add ph, gh or qu in the space to make a word that matches the definition.

1. _____artz hard rock
2. dol_____in sea creature
3. nei_____ noise of a horse
4. be_____est gift
5. plou_____ farm implement
6. al_____abet letters of our language
7. _____obia great fear
8. _____adrangle four-sided area
9. slei_____ snow vehicle
10. gra_____ data format
11. trou_____ drinking container
12. _____arrel argument, fight

Parent/Teacher Signature Date

UNIT 44

Test 1

The underlined word in each sentence is incorrectly spelled. Write it correctly at the end of the sentence.

1	The prisoner was found giltey of murder.	1
2	Ethan will attend primery school soon.	2
3	I moved the cursar on the computer.	3
4	The large tracter pulled the plough.	4
5	The dentist extracted the man's moler.	5
6	He was awarded a trofy for his good play.	6
7	The English alfabet has twenty-six letters.	7
8	We were given a large qantity of food.	8
9	The road was made form crushed quortz.	9
10	This steak is so tuff my knife can't cut it.	10
11	I bought lollies and other confectionary from the shop.	11
12	The government will conduct a sensus next year.	12
13	This diamond is jenuine and not artificial.	13
14	She has a real fobia about spiders.	14
15	The car raced quickly around the sircuit.	15

Total correct ______ / 15

Parent/Teacher Signature   Date

Test 2

Choose the correct spelling of the word in the brackets.

1	Ducks, geese and fowls are called (poltri, poultry, pultry).	1
2	We need (oxigen, oxygen, oxyjen) to breathe.	2
3	I saw my image in the (mirror, mirra, mirrer).	3
4	The (couga, couger, cougar) stalked its prey cleverly.	4
5	The ship dropped (ankor, ancher, anchor) in the harbour.	5
6	They crushed the rock into a (powder, powdor, powda).	6
7	He marked a (hyphen, hifen, hyfen) in his book.	7
8	I bought the pills at the (farmacy, pharmacy, pharmace).	8
9	The teacher (tort, taugt, taught) us about dinosaurs.	9
10	Their singing group is a (quintet, qintet, quintat).	10
11	I enjoy (sereal, cereal, cerial) for breakfast.	11
12	The (gorilla, gorila, goorila) was taken to a zoo.	12
13	The seeds will (jerminate, germineight, germinate) soon.	13
14	I am (sertain, surtain, certain) she did it.	14
15	The clown made us (laugh, laff, larf) till we cried.	15

Total correct ______
15

Parent/Teacher Signature Date

Adding ion to base words

To add the suffix **ion** to different words, follow this guide:

★ For words that end in **ct**, **ss** or **t**, simply add the **ion**, as in **extinction**, **expression** and **deduction**.

★ For words that end in **de**, change the **de** to an **s** and add **ion** (**deride**, **derision**).

★ For words that end in **e**, drop the **e** and then add **ion** (**educate**, **education**).

Make each word in brackets end in **ion** to complete the sentences below. Change the spelling of the base word if it is needed.

1. This is a difficult ________________. (subtract)
2. To correct the article the editor made a ________________. (delete)
3. The ________________ of the food took over a day. (digest)
4. There was a ________________ on the highway last night. (collide)
5. There has been a lot of wind ________________ here. (erode)
6. Finishing the job gave him a sense of ________________. (complete)
7. A loud ________________ rocked the city last night. (explode)
8. I got all the ________________ sums correct. (divide)
9. The large street ________________ was enjoyed by all. (process)
10. The man's leg has a severe ________________. (infect)
11. Her ________________ of the story was perfect. (narrate)
12. This is an extremely clever ________________. (invent)
13. The ________________ of the essay improved it immensely. (revise)
14. The ________________ by the army began yesterday. (invade)
15. The worker's ________________ was very useful. (suggest)
16. It will take much ________________ to get her to agree. (persuade)

Write these words in sentences of your own:

incision ____

abrasion ____

Parent/Teacher Signature   Date

Adding able to base words

UNIT 47

To add the suffix **able** to base words, follow this guide:

★ For many words, no spelling changes are necessary. Example: expand + **able** = expandable

★ For most words that end in **e**, drop the **e** and add **able**.

Example: adore + **able** = adorable

★ However, words that end in **e** following the consonants **c** or **g**, usually retain the **e**. Example: enforce + **able** = enforceable

Make the base words in the brackets end in **able** and write them in the spaces.

1. His poor efforts were quite ________________. (laugh)
2. In early England some petty crimes were ________________ by death. (punish)
3. This is an extremely ________________ watch. (value)
4. The change in her behaviour has been quite ________________. (notice)
5. To win the first prize would be ________________. (desire)
6. This is a very ________________ lounge suit. (comfort)
7. These new shoes are quite ________________. (afford)
8. The weather has been very ________________. (change)
9. His story was really quite ________________. (believe)
10. It is not ________________ that he was the only one to make it. (conceive)
11. These foods are ________________ to those fatty ones. (prefer)
12. The accident was really quite ________________. (avoid)
13. It is ________________ whether he should have received the prize. (debate)
14. I am afraid those rules are simply not ________________. (enforce)
15. The new puppies were really quite ________________. (love)
16. His performances have been ________________ lately. (remark)

Write these words in sentences of your own:

liveable ____

transferable ____

Parent/Teacher Signature Date

UNIT 48

Doubling with absorbed prefixes

When adding a prefix we often double letters. This has come about often to make pronunciation easier. For example, the prefix in **opposition** originally came from **ob** but because the root word **position** begins with **p** the prefix **op** was used to make it easier to pronounce.

Each word in the box contains a prefix. Write each word in its correct sentence.

approximately	**supplement**	**attention**	**aggravate**
assemble	**surrender**	**acceptable**	**allowance**
arrogant	**succumbed**	**accomplish**	**apprehend**
effigy	**committee**	**accelerate**	**appetite**

1. The children made an _______________ of Guy Fawkes for the bonfire.
2. The soldiers decided to _______________ as they were so exhausted.
3. We ate some bread to _______________ our meal.
4. The students paid _______________ to the speech.
5. We hope to _______________ many things this year.
6. Do not rub that cut or you will _______________ the injury.
7. The police will _______________ the burglar soon.
8. All the students were ordered to _______________.
9. The new school principal is quite _______________ and strict.
10. He finally _______________ to the pressure and agreed.
11. Jess has a large _______________ for any kind of sweet food.
12. The football club _______________ has ten members.
13. After the police car passed the car began to _______________.
14. My parents gave me an _______________ of pocket money each week.
15. His poor behaviour was definitely not _______________ at school.
16. It was _______________ 10 am when the accident happened.

Write these words in sentences of your own:

alleviate ____

correspond ____

Parent/Teacher Signature Date

The word ending ure

The word ending **ure** can be pronounced with a hard **y** sound, as in **failure**, or a soft schwa sound, as in **pleasure**.

These words all end in **ure** but their pronunciation differs slightly. Say each word to yourself and then write it in the correct sentence below.

assure	**endure**	**leisure**	**composure**
pressure	**failure**	**pleasure**	**enclosure**
brochure	**obscure**	**treasure**	**closure**
exposure	**manicure**	**procedure**	**insecure**

1. The film star has had a lot of __________________ in the media.
2. She decided to have a luxurious __________________ as a treat.
3. Having cosmetic surgery can be a complicated __________________.
4. We felt __________________ on the ride because the seats were rusty.
5. The __________________ of the restaurant was disappointing.
6. We asked the travel firm to send us a __________________ on Vietnam.
7. There was a lot of __________________ on the students to be successful.
8. I can __________________ you the principal will be back tomorrow.
9. She had to __________________ cruel remarks from her classmates.
10. His __________________ to win the race surprised us all.
11. The mountains are quite __________________ in this fog.
12. We work during the weekdays but have __________________ time on the weekends.
13. I got a lot of __________________ in seeing her so happy again.
14. The pirates buried their __________________ under the rocks.
15. The wild animals were kept in a wired __________________.
16. He displayed __________________ and courage in the circumstances.

Write these words in sentences of your own:

secure ____

injure ____

conjure ____

Parent/Teacher Signature Date

UNIT 50

Revision

A Make the words in the brackets end in **ion**. Make any spelling changes necessary.

1. a useful ________________ (invent)
2. a loud ________________ (explode)
3. a good ________________ (impress)
4. a painful ________________ (inject)
5. a quick ________________ (act)
6. a happy ________________ (conclude)
7. a violent ________________ (object)
8. increased ________________ (product)
9. a novel ________________ (distract)
10. a sincere ________________ (confess)
11. destructive ________________ (erode)
12. an exact ________________ (imitate)

B Make these words end in **able**. Make any spelling changes necessary.

1. most ________________ (afford)
2. very ________________ (predict)
3. easily ________________ (identify)
4. very ________________ (adore)
5. very ________________ (admire)
6. easily ________________ (manage)
7. easily ________________ (notice)
8. very ________________ (profit)
9. very ________________ (depend)
10. often ________________ (change)
11. very ________________ (excite)
12. least ________________ (value)

C From the words in the box find the word ending in **ure** that best fills each space below.

failure	**enclosure**	**obscure**	**adventure**	**procedure**
treasure	**mature**	**brochure**	**pressure**	**manicure**

1. a wire ________________
2. a fingernail ________________
3. buried ________________
4. an ________________ idea
5. high air ________________
6. an exciting ________________
7. a difficult ________________
8. an informative ________________
9. a dismal ________________
10. a ________________ adult

Parent/Teacher Signature Date

Test

One word in each sentence is spelled wrongly. Write the correct spelling of the word on the line at the end of the sentence.

1	We had an interesting diskussion about school.	1
2	He made a sensible sugestion.	2
3	This is a valuble watch.	3
4	I'm afraid that rule would not be enforsable.	4
5	What a remarkible achievement.	5
6	I hope we akomplesh all we set out to do.	6
7	They burned the ephigy in the bonfire.	7
8	He felt very insekure in the strange city.	8
9	There was a lot of water preshure in the tap.	9
10	It was a stupid iresponsible act.	10
11	Oliver is always very exitable.	11
12	The fundraiser was very profetible.	12
13	The new worker made a good immpression on the boss.	13
14	It is ilegal to drive a car if you are only twelve.	14
15	We got a great deal of plessure from the holiday.	15

Total correct ______
15

Parent/Teacher Signature Date

UNIT 52

Base word plus suffix

Suffixes are groups of letters added to the end of a word. They often complete the meaning of the word, as in the examples below.

capable of: able, ible	person: ary	place of action: ory
descriptive: ane, ery, ive, ile	diminutive: ette, ule	abstract noun: ment
belonging to: ary, ic, ine	condition: tude	agent: ant

A Add a suffix from the box to complete each word below. Note the meaning.

1. He works as a shop assist________ in the centre of town.
2. We did not appreciate her arrogant atti________.
3. The physicist was a real vision________ in regards to scientific progress.
4. It is necess________ to get a licence before driving a car.
5. It is dangerous to smoke that cigar________.
6. These thin metal rods are quite flex________.
7. She is an extremely happy and ami________ person.
8. It was a hum________ gesture to let the captives go free.
9. This new crane in the city is gigant________.
10. The escaped fugit________ was soon caught.
11. The terrier is a species of can________.
12. The children were told to choose a bed each in the dormit________.
13. The molec________ contained two atoms.
14. Be careful as that thin glass is very frag________.
15. The elderly man is having an enjoyable retire________ from his work.
16. We purchased some buns at the bak________.

B Add a suffix from the box to complete the words below.

ate	ee	al	ice	ior	ent
(verb)	(person)	(belonging to)	(abstract noun)	(more)	(full of)

1. absent____________
2. just____________
3. renov____________
4. inter____________
5. roy____________
6. viol____________

Parent/Teacher Signature Date

Base word plus prefix

A prefix is a group of letters added to the beginning of a word to alter its meaning. For spelling there are no changes needed. A prefix is simply added. Examples: **in** + visible = invisible; **un** + necessary = unnecessary

A In the box are some prefixes with their meanings. Add the correct prefix to each word in the brackets to complete the sentences below.

anti = against	mis = wrong	auto = self	bi = two
in = not	ex = out of	dis = not (negative)	extra = beyond

1. The film star wrote her _______________ in the book. (graph)
2. Sally has _______________ all her study sheets. (placed)
3. The doctor administered the _______________ to the sick person. (dote)
4. The planes became _______________ through the clouds. (visible)
5. We _______________ a lot of coal and iron ore from Australia to Japan. (port)
6. Mia rode a _______________ to school yesterday. (cycle)
7. They believed they had seen an ____________________ landing. (terrestrial)
8. Tom's poor grades continue to _______________ him. (courage)

B On the left-hand side are some Latin prefixes along with their meanings. Add the prefix to the word stems on the right to make complete words.

bene = well
bis or **bi** = two
circum = round
de = down, away
dis = negative or apart
ex = out of
extra = beyond
intro = into
non = not

1. ________navigate
2. ________locate
3. ________factor
4. ________cycle
5. ________fit
6. ________plode
7. ________terrestial
8. ________smoking
9. ________cuit
10. ________able
11. ________pose
12. ________sense
13. ________duce
14. ________perse
15. ________pel
16. ________ordinary

Parent/Teacher Signature　　　　　　　　　　Date

Foreign words and phrases

In English we use many foreign words and phrases we should be able to spell.

A Match the meanings in the box to the foreign words or phrases underlined in the sentences below.

a. desire to travel (G)	g. social error (Fr)	l. openness (R)
b. final blow (Fr)	h. solid ground (L)	m. about, approximately (L)
c. go with God (S)	i. restructuring (R)	n. method of operation (L)
d. joy of living (Fr)	j. pen name (Fr)	o. excessive sentimentality (Y)
e. unknown territory (L)	k. showpiece item (Fr)	p. dangerous woman (Fr)
f. peace to you (Ar)	Key: Fr = French, G = German, S = Spanish, L = Latin, Ar = Arabic, R = Russian, Y = Yiddish	

1. James Bond, Agent 007, had many dealings with a femme fatale (Fr). ___
2. The events occurred circa (L) 200 BC. ___
3. The victor gave the fallen knight his coup de grace (Fr). ___
4. When she was at the mayoral ball she made a faux pas (Fr). ___
5. When the plane finally landed I was glad to be on terra firma (L). ___
6. As we parted he called vaya con Dios (S) to me. ___
7. During the interview he revealed his modus operandi (L). ___
8. Chloe has a lot of joie de vivre (F) today.___
9. Our company is undergoing a period of perestroika (R). ___
10. The famous author wrote under a nom de plume (Fr). ___
11. The movie contained nothing but schmaltz (Y), which I hated. ___
12. I warn you that you are entering terra incognita (L). ___
13. The world is now beginning a period of general glasnost (R). ___
14. Among her many pieces the blue one is her piece de resistance (Fr). ___
15. My Egyptian friend called asalaam alaykum (Ar) to me. ___
16. My brother has real wanderlust (G). ___

B Match these foreign phrases to their meanings.

1. persona non grata (L) ☐
2. nota bene (L) ☐
3. alma mater (L) ☐
4. anno Domini (L) ☐
5. enfant terrible (F) ☐
6. caveat emptor (L) ☐

a. let the buyer beware	c. old school	e. note well
b. in the year of our Lord	d. unwanted person	f. naughty child

Parent/Teacher Signature   Date

Complex consonant groups, ch and tch

A The letters **ch** are usually pronounced as a **ch** sound, as in **cheap** and **peach**, but sometimes as a **k** sound, as in **scheme** and **orchestra**. Find the **ch** words in the grid and write them in the correct spaces.

b	r	o	o	c	h	c	o
p	o	a	c	h	a	r	r
c	o	a	c	h	t	o	c
b	e	a	c	h	t	u	h
p	o	u	c	h	a	c	a
b	i	r	c	h	c	h	r
c	o	u	c	h	h	x	d

1. When it's hot we go to the ____________ to play.
2. She had to ____________ down to pat the puppy.
3. We picked the apricots in the ____________.
4. A large ____________ tree grew in the yard.
5. She wore a pretty ____________ on her coat.
6. She lazed on the ____________ all afternoon.
7. The magnet will ____________ itself to the iron bar.
8. Our soccer ____________ told us to try harder.
9. A kangaroo has a ____________ for its joey.
10. Today I learned how to ____________ an egg.

B The letters **tch** are pronounced the same as the **ch** sound, as in **hatch**. Write each **tch** word from the box beside its meaning below.

dispatch	**sketch**	**butterscotch**	**hopscotch**	**kitchen**	**witch**
watch	**clutch**	**britches**	**ketch**	**satchel**	**latch**

1. small ship ________________
2. to send ________________
3. hopping game ________________
4. mythical evil woman ________________
5. part of a lock ________________
6. kind of sweet ________________
7. cooking room ________________
8. trousers ________________
9. part of a car's gear system ________________
10. small timepiece ________________
11. quick drawing ________________
12. leather bag ________________

Write these words in sentences of your own:

speech ____

stretch ____

twitch ____

Parent/Teacher Signature Date

UNIT 56

Final unstressed syllables, al, il and ile

Final unstressed syllables such as al (**final**) and il (**fossil**) have no distinct vowel sound. However, the final syllable ile (**hostile**), while still unstressed, is pronounced with a long i sound.

Look closely at the words in the box. Write each in its correct sentence below.

fatal	**vandal**	**peril**	**missile**
mammal	**final**	**nostril**	**mobile**
central	**educational**	**fossil**	**hostile**
sandal	**cymbal**	**docile**	**sterile**

1. A __________ is a creature that feeds its young on milk.
2. This is the __________ time I will explain what to do.
3. The __________ on his right foot has a broken strap.
4. These __________ toys help youngsters a lot.
5. He plays the __________ in the orchestra.
6. The __________ did a lot of damage to the building.
7. A __________ accident occurred at the crossroads.
8. The shop is in the __________ part of the city.
9. The geologist studied the animal __________ carefully.
10. That __________ carries a nuclear warhead.
11. The people were __________ towards the unexpected visitors.
12. The scalpel must be __________ before the operation begins.
13. The young swimmmer did not realise the great __________ she was facing.
14. The wild horse is now __________ as it has been fed well.
15. I called my friend on my __________ telephone.
16. The girl's __________ became painful from sneezing.

Write these words in sentences of your own:

metal __________

pupil __________

fragile __________

Parent/Teacher Signature Date

Final unstressed syllables, el and le

The final unstressed syllables **el** (**label**) and **le** (**bottle**) have no distinct vowel sound.

A Find all the **el** words in the grid and write them beside their meaning.

a	j	e	w	e	l	k	c
a	a	n	g	e	l	e	h
b	l	a	b	e	l	n	a
s	h	o	v	e	l	n	p
b	a	r	r	e	l	e	e
d	i	e	s	e	l	l	l
q	u	a	r	r	e	l	x

1. garden tool ____________________
2. fuel for engine ____________________
3. heavenly spirit ____________________
4. dog's home ____________________
5. small church ____________________
6. precious gem ____________________
7. container for water ____________________
8. argument, petty fight ____________________
9. descriptive tag ____________________

B Look closely at the **le** words in the box and then write each beside a word it can be linked to in some way below.

saddle	**rectangle**	**chuckle**	**bramble**	**cradle**	**kettle**
knuckle	**dribble**	**beagle**	**ankle**	**bugle**	**needle**

1. basketball ____________________
2. fist ____________________
3. laugh ____________________
4. bush ____________________
5. horse ____________________
6. dog ____________________
7. foot ____________________
8. baby ____________________
9. shape ____________________
10. sewing ____________________
11. tea ____________________
12. brass ____________________

Write these words in sentences of your own:

morsel ____

cuddle ____

grumble ____

Parent/Teacher Signature   Date

UNIT 58

Final unstressed syllables, et and it

Final unstressed syllables such as **et** (**cricket**) and **it** (**profit**) have no distinct vowel sound.

A These **et** words are cramped together. Find the words and write them beside the correct meanings below.

faucetcarpetcrickethatchethornettablettrumpetvelvetwalletjacketcometbas-ket

1. floor covering ________________
2. small axe ________________
3. pill for illness ________________
4. soft material ________________
5. light coat ________________
6. picnic container ________________
7. American word for tap ________________
8. sport ________________
9. stinging insect ________________
10. musical instrument ________________
11. container for paper money ________________
12. space object ________________

B Find the **it** words in the grid and write them in the spaces to complete the sentences.

b	a	n	d	i	t
o	p	r	s	h	c
r	r	a	u	e	r
b	o	b	m	r	e
i	f	b	m	m	d
t	i	i	i	i	i
x	t	t	t	t	t

1. The school fair made a large ________________.
2. On reaching the ________________ the climbers rested.
3. My bank account has a large ________________ balance.
4. The ________________ held up the stagecoach.
5. The ________________ ran for the safety of its burrow.
6. The satellite is in ________________ around the moon.
7. The ________________ did not like the arrival of the visitors.

Write these words in sentences of your own:

helmet ________________________________

puppet ________________________________

audit ________________________________

limit ________________________________

Parent/Teacher Signature Date

Long vowel sounds

A long vowel sound says its letter name.
Examples: **ape** and **cute**

A Write each word in the correct space below.

crayon	**donate**	**spider**	**tulip**	**cleaner**
pavement	**hopeful**	**silent**	**bugle**	**cheetah**

1. The car skidded across the road onto the ________________.
2. The wealthy man likes to ________________ funds to the hospital.
3. The tiger was ________________ as it stalked its prey.
4. The ________________ asked us to help tidy the room.
5. The fastest of all land creatures is the ________________.
6. The child drew a picture using the ________________.
7. I am ________________ that our team will win this week.
8. The ________________ made its web between the twigs.
9. She played the ________________ in the army band.
10. Mike put the ________________ in the vase.

B Write each word from the box in the correct space below.

decay	**approach**	**reptile**	**utility**	**compete**
terrain	**explode**	**surprise**	**perfume**	**disease**

1. The people were inoculated to prevent the spread of the ________________.
2. A snake is a ________________ without any legs.
3. The dentist warned her about the ________________ in her tooth.
4. Be careful you don't drop the bomb as it may ________________.
5. The ______________ of the area made our progress up the mountain difficult.
6. He got a ________________ when he saw all his friends at the party.
7. The sweet-smelling ________________ attracted the insects.
8. The puppies began to ________________ for their mother's affection.
9. They drove the ________________ to the nearby river.
10. You must be wary when you ________________ a wild dingo.

Parent/Teacher Signature Date

UNIT 60

Silent letters

Many words have letters that are not sounded. There are historical reasons for the inclusion of these letters and once many of them were sounded. These silent, or unsounded, letters can be consonants (the **g** in **gnaw**) or vowels (the **a** in **tread**).

A Each word in the box has a silent letter. Write the correct word beside its meaning below and circle the silent letter.

autumn	**hymn**	**pneumonia**	**knife**
sword	**choir**	**handsome**	**rhubarb**
beret	**knuckle**	**dinghy**	**scent**

1. red-stalked plant ______________.
2. cutting tool ______________
3. season ______________
4. soft cap ______________
5. singing group ______________
6. steel weapon ______________
7. lung disease ______________
8. perfume ______________
9. good looking ______________
10. small rubber boat ______________
11. finger joint ______________
12. sacred song ______________

B Each of these words is missing a silent letter. Write the word correctly.

1. dout ______________
2. gost ______________
3. thum ______________
4. casle ______________
5. plumer ______________
6. lam ______________
7. sissors ______________
8. Wenesday ______________
9. cemical ______________
10. ofen ______________
11. nife ______________
12. det ______________

C Circle the silent vowel in each word.

1. head 2. touch 3. young 4. enough 5. bread 6. trouble 7. guard 8. thread

D Circle the silent consonant in each word.

1. wriggle 2. thistle 3. solemn 4. scent 5. campaign 6. sign 7. knelt 8. depot

Parent/Teacher Signature Date

Revision

A Make these words end in **al**, **il** or **ile**.

1. cryst____ (hard rock)
2. penc____ (writing implement)
3. fert____ (rich soil)
4. ped____ (part of bike)
5. pup____ (part of eye)
6. frag____ (easily broken)
7. journ____ (magazine)
8. fut____ (hopeless)
9. per____ (danger)
10. host____ (angry, threatening)
11. lent____ (legume)
12. pet____ (part of a flower)

B Make these words end in **el** or **le**.

1. mors____ (scrap of food)
2. rectang____ (four-sided shape)
3. parc____ (package)
4. knuck____ (part of a fist)
5. hov____ (poor-standard dwelling)
6. kenn____ (dog's home)
7. quarr____ (argument)
8. ming____ (mix with others)
9. mirac____ (amazing happening)
10. crumb____ (break into crumbs)
11. past____ (drawing implement)
12. comp____ (force)

C Make these words end in **et** or **it**.

1. helm____ (hard headwear)
2. rabb____ (small furry animal)
3. jack____ (light coat)
4. summ____ (top of a mountain)
5. hab____ (repeated behaviour)
6. targ____ (what you aim to hit)
7. scarl____ (bright red colour)
8. aud____ (accounts check)
9. blank____ (bed covering)
10. spir____ (alcoholic drink)
11. buck____ (container for water)
12. dig____ (number, toe or finger)

Parent/Teacher Signature Date

Test 1

Choose the correct spelling of the word in brackets and write it correctly in the space.

1	A possum has a (powch, pouch, poush).	1
2	We cooked the meal in the (kitchen, kikchen, kichen).	2
3	An (orchid, orkid, owkid) is a beautiful flower.	3
4	The scientist studied the (fosill, fossel, fossil).	4
5	This book is (educational, edgeucation, educationael).	5
6	A (mammal, mammel, mamil) feeds its young on milk.	6
7	We kept the wine in a wooden (barel, barrol, barrel).	7
8	She tripped and injured her (ankle, ancle, ankel).	8
9	The baby is asleep in the (cradel, cradle, craydle).	9
10	A (hachit, hatchit, hatchet) is a small axe.	10
11	The (rabit, rabbet, rabbit) ran to its burrow.	11
12	I kept the notes in my (wollat, wallit, wallet).	12
13	This orange (juice, jooce, juise) is sweet.	13
14	I got a (serprise, surpise, surprise) when he arrived.	14
15	In the (ballot, ballat, ballit) he got the most votes.	15

Total correct ________
15

Parent/Teacher Signature   Date

Test 2

In each sentence one word is spelled incorrectly. Find the incorrect word and write it on the line.

1	Sally hopes to one day be a fashion modal.	1
2	A lot of peepel were at the party.	2
3	The magnat stuck to the iron.	3
4	In the band she plays the trumpit.	4
5	The author has written a sequil to this book.	5
6	The material is now sterrile.	6
7	A large expensive jowel was in the glass cabinet.	7
8	He felt so sick he thought he might vommet.	8
9	The coast was hit by a tidel wave.	9
10	Mike lives in the city but Jan lives in a rurel area.	10
11	He is a member of the city councel.	11
12	I stuck a lable on the case.	12
13	I'm sure there will be ampel room for us all.	13
14	The miners were looking for nickle.	14
15	He would simply whistel to get the dogs to come.	15

Total correct ______ / 15

Parent/Teacher Signature Date

UNIT 64

Past tense, regular verbs

Verbs have three tenses — present, past and future (**I like, I liked, I will like**). Many spelling errors are caused by the difficulty we sometimes have in changing the tense of words.

A common way of forming the past tense is to add **ed** (**scream, screamed**). However, when a word ends in **y**, you change the **y** to **i** before adding **ed** (**rely, relied**). For some words, you double the last letter before adding the **ed** (**hop, hopped**). These are called regular verbs.

A Write the past tense of the words in brackets to complete the sentences below.

1. Our team easily ________________ our opponents. (defeat)
2. At lunch I cut the potatoes while Sam ________________ the meat. (prepare)
3. I didn't hear what she said so she ________________ herself. (repeat)
4. The drover ________________ for his dogs to come. (whistle)
5. Because it was so hot and steamy we ________________ a great deal. (perspire)
6. Yesterday a young boy nearly ________________ in the pool. (drown)
7. The car ________________ across the icy road. (skid)
8. The girls ________________ by bus to the city. (travel)
9. The tap ________________ constantly last night. (drip)
10. Michelle ________________ the sugar into her tea. (stir)
11. The frightened prisoner ________________ his captors for mercy. (beg)
12. Yesterday the dog ________________ the bone in the yard. (bury)
13. This morning I ________________ Sophie's homework sheet. (copy)
14. The burglar ________________ taking the jewel. (deny)
15. Last year the insects in this area ________________ greatly. (multiply)
16. The new house is presently ________________ by foreigners. (occupy)

B Change these words to past tense and write them in sentences:

1. stop ____

2. hurry ____

Parent/Teacher Signature Date

Past tense, irregular verbs

Verbs have three tenses — present, past and future (**I play, I played, I will play**). The past tense of many words causes difficulties in spelling. This is particularly so with those that change one or more letters. These are irregular verbs.

Example: Today I ring the bell. Yesterday I rang the bell.

A Write the past tense of the words in brackets to complete the sentences below.

1. Yesterday I ________________ the paper into thin strips. (tear)
2. This morning I ________________ ill at school. (become)
3. When I was hit this morning my nose ________________ a lot. (bleed)
4. Paul ________________ his father's car yesterday. (drive)
5. Last night I ________________ quite ill after eating the fish. (fall)
6. It was so cold the water ________________ in the taps. (freeze)
7. The player was ________________ on the nose by a bat. (strike)
8. I ________________ the toys from the children last week. (take)
9. The teacher ________________ to Mia about her good results. (speak)
10. The detectives ________________ answers to the crime. (seek)
11. Last night a thief ________________ my wallet. (steal)
12. In the movie the boy ________________ a donkey into town. (ride)
13. The choir ________________ the song sweetly. (sing)
14. Yesterday our teacher ________________ us about the need for good hygiene. (teach)
15. The frightened mouse ________________ quietly out of its hole. (creep)
16. The soldiers ________________ bravely in the last battle. (fight)

B Complete the past tense of these phrases:

Today ...	Yesterday ...	Today ...	Yesterday ...
1. I deal	I ________________	5. I eat	I ________________
2. I break	I ________________	6. I flee	I ________________
3. I begin	I ________________	7. I drink	I ________________
4. I blow	I ________________	8. I am	I ________________

Parent/Teacher Signature Date

UNIT 66

Comparisons

Adjectives have three forms of comparison – positive, comparative and superlative. Example: big, bigger, biggest

When you compare two things you can add er without altering the spelling of many words (**tall, taller, tallest**). If the word ends in e, drop the e to add ed or est (**large, larger, largest**).

If the word ends in y, change the y to i before adding er or est (**heavy, heavier, heaviest**).

For words that end with a short vowel and a consonant, double the last letter before adding the er or est (**wet, wetter, wettest**).

For words of three or more syllables, instead of adding er or est, use the words **more** or **most**. Example: beautiful, more beautiful, most beautiful

Complete the sentences below by adding the correct comparison of the word in brackets.

1. This church is much ________________ than that one. (old)
2. Mike is __________________ then Billy. (tall)
3. Billy is __________________ than I am. (clever)
4. The light in my room is __________________ than those in the kitchen. (bright)
5. Jack's decision was ________________ than Joanne's. (wise)
6. The particles of powder in this jar are ______________ than yours. (fine)
7. These pipes are ___________________ than that lot. (heavy)
8. Bill is always __________________ than I am. (lucky)
9. The water in the jug is _____________ than that in the tap. (hot)
10. I think Sally is ___________________ than the film star. (pretty)
11. This patient can wait because he is ___________________ than the old man. (healthy)
12. These clothes are _________________ than those shirts. (dry)
13. These dogs are ___________________ than those terriers. (big)
14. I feel ___________________ than a king today. (happy)
15. Our class is ___________________ than the one next door. (noisy)
16. Ella can be ___________________ than anyone else in class. (nasty)

Parent/Teacher Signature   Date

Adding ance and ence to base words

The suffixes **ance** and **ence** are often used to change adjectives and verbs to abstract nouns. Example: fragrant (adjective), fragrance (abstract noun)

Sometimes, however, the spelling of the base word also changes. Examples: enter, entrance; defy, defiance

Change the words in brackets to an **ance** or **ence** ending and write it in the space.

1. The actor gave a stunning ________________ in her latest role. (perform)
2. She sent the ________________ card almost immediately. (accept)
3. She entered the room with great ________________. (elegant)
4. His constant ________________ was envied by others. (extravagant)
5. The ________________ of the roses could be smelled from across the room. (fragrant)
6. His ________________ was greatly appreciated by the others. (assist)
7. The family's ________________ is in this street. (resident)
8. A lot of ________________ has occurred in our city recently. (violent)
9. The film star made sure her ________________ was noticed by all. (enter)
10. The ________________ of the occasion was noted. (important)
11. His ________________ in this matter is a disappointment to us all. (ignore)
12. The ________________ for this gem is more than its value. (insure)
13. The ________________ of native grasses in this bushland is very pleasing. (abundant)
14. The ________________ between the two cities is not that far. (distant)
15. The boy's ________________ in sport is outstanding. (competent)
16. There is a lot of ________________ between the two siblings. (different)

Write these words in sentences of your own:

reluctance ____

radiance ____

patience ____

dependence ____

Parent/Teacher Signature Date

UNIT 68

Revision

A Write the correct words in the space.

Today I . . .	Yesterday I . . .	Today I . . .	Yesterday I . . .
1. play	____________	6. freeze	____________
2. write	____________	7. ____________	bled
3. cry	____________	8. steal	____________
4. ____________	sought	9. ____________	broke
5. ____________	crept	10. ____________	fled

A Find the words in the grid and turn them into comparisons to complete the sentences.

f	a	t	d	r	y
p	r	e	t	t	y
w	i	s	e	s	h
l	u	c	k	y	o
n	o	i	s	y	t

1. I think Lily is ____________ than a picture.
2. Our teacher is ____________ than any of us.
3. Your old car is ____________ than our new car.
4. The pig is ____________ than the thin dog.
5. It is ____________ today than yesterday.
6. This shirt is ____________ than that wet one.
7. Joshua is ____________ than I am in raffles.

C Add **ance** or **ence** to complete each word.

1. It was time the youth showed some independ________.
2. His resist________ to our ideas amazed us.
3. The brilli________ of the lights blinded us.
4. The dog's obedi________ is without question.
5. The innoc________ of the youth was soon proven.
6. There was a big differ________ in size between the two.
7. The customers impati________ to be served angered the assistant.
8. The relev________ of his work is questionable.
9. The girl displayed a lot of exuber________ towards the idea.
10. The evid________ of the witness swayed the jury.

Parent/Teacher Signature Date

Test

Choose the correct spellings from the words in the brackets to complete the sentences.

1	The dog (buryed, buried) the bone in the garden.	1
2	An accident (occurred, occured) at the crossroads.	2
3	The microbes in the old milk (multiplied, multiplyed) quickly.	3
4	Chloe (stired, stirred) the contents of the pot.	4
5	The boy (drowned, drownded) yesterday.	5
6	The choir (sung, sang) the song sweetly.	6
7	This star is (brighter, briter) than that one.	7
8	My guinea pig is (after, fatter) than yours.	8
9	This rash is (nastyier, nastier) than the other boy's.	9
10	Lachlan is always (luckier, luckyar) than I am.	10
11	The feed is (abundant, abundent) in this paddock.	11
12	There is a lot of (difference, diffrence) between the sisters.	12
13	His (ignorence, ignorance) of the subject is appalling.	13
14	There has been a lot of (violence, violance) lately.	14
15	She gave a shining (performence, performance).	15

Total correct ______
15

Parent/Teacher Signature Date

UNIT 70

Homophones

Homophones are words that sound the same but have different spellings and different meanings. They are a type of homonym.

Choose the correct word from the box to fill the spaces below.

bridle	**formally**	**holy**	**lesson**	**morning**	**principle**	**taught**	**moose**
bridal	**formerly**	**wholly**	**lessen**	**mourning**	**principal**	**taut**	**mousse**

1. When I got up this ________________ it was raining heavily.
2. The teacher gave us a ________________ on first aid.
3. This stone in the shape of a crucifix is said to be ________________.
4. The principal conducted the interviews ________________.
5. The jockey tightened the ________________ on the horse.
6. The large ________________ aimed its antlers and ran at the wolves.
7. We were ________________ a good lesson never to miss school again.
8. The scientist explained the ________________ of how the machine worked.
9. The ________________ party left for the wedding reception.
10. The mayor was ________________ a teacher at our school.
11. The strong winds began to ________________ in ferocity.
12. The wires between the posts are quite ________________.
13. The ________________ of our school addressed the staff at lunchtime.
14. This company is ________________ owned by people from overseas.
15. I chose some chocolate ________________ for dessert.
16. The whole town is in ________________ for the loss of their hero.

Write these words in sentences of your own:

idle ____

idol ____

cereal ____

serial ____

Parent/Teacher Signature   Date

Change of meaning by stress

UNIT 71

Stressed syllables have a distinct vowel sound. For example, the first syllable in **label** is stressed and has the long **a** vowel sound, while the second is unstressed and has the schwa sound.

The words in the box change their meaning with a shift of stress between the first and second syllables. These words are homographs, which have the same spellings but are pronounced differently. The underlined part of the word is the syllable that is stressed.

Write each word in its correct space, underlining the stressed syllable. Say the words aloud as you do this.

in/val/id re/cord pre/sent re/fuse min/ute con/vict
in/val/id rec/ord pres/ent ref/use mi/nute con/vict

1. (a) The elderly ______________ was cared for at the local hospital.
   (b) You cannot come in as your pass is out of date and is ______________.
2. (a) The captain of the team will ______________ the awards tonight.
   (b) I gave Billy a computer game as a birthday ______________.
3. (a) An atom is a ______________ particle of matter.
   (b) She will complete the whole course in under a ______________.
4. (a) The band is going to ______________ its greatest hit.
   (b) Tom holds the ______________ for the long jump at our school.
5. (a) The police will try to ______________ him of the crime.
   (b) The ______________ was given ten lashes of the cat-o'-nine tails.
6. (a) I'm afraid I will have to ______________ your kind invitation.
   (b) The potato peels and other ______________ were thrown on the garden.

Write these words in sentences of your own:

ob/ject ____

ob/ject ____

Parent/Teacher Signature Date

Origin of words

Many words have an interesting origin. Can you work out what each word is from the given clue?

1. Jean Nicot introduced tobacco into France.

   ____

2. A knife attached to a rifle was invented in Bayonne, France.

   ____

3. Louis Pasteur invented a way to sterilise milk.

   ____

4. The Latin word minitus meant small.

   ____

5. Ceres was the mythical goddess of corn.

   ____

6. Dr Joseph Guillotin invented a decapitating machine.

   ____

7. A flower got its name from the French word d'ent de lion, which means tooth of a lion.

   ____

8. Oporto in Portugal is famous for a special type of wine.

   ____

9. Early people counted with stones and the Latin word for pebbles is calculus.

   ____

10. A small orange fruit comes from Tangiers in Morocco.

    ____

11. The Rugby School in England developed a football game.

    ____

12. The Earl of Sandwich developed a new way to serve food.

    ____

dandelion	**tangerine**	**bayonet**	**pasteurise**
minute	**guillotine**	**rugby**	**nicotine**
cereal	**calculator**	**sandwich**	**port**

Parent/Teacher Signature　　　　　　　　　　Date

Review

A Sort these words by the sound of the first letter, under the headings below.

cider	**carpet**	**celery**	**confectionery**
genius	**genuine**	**guilty**	**glacier**
cuckoo	**guitar**	**geology**	**gymnasium**
gadget	**cyclone**	**cucumber**	**circle**

Hard c sound	Soft c sound	Hard g sound	Soft g sound
________	________	________	________
________	________	________	________
________	________	________	________
________	________	________	________

B Make these words end in **able**.

1. ________ crime (punish)
2. ________ dress (afford)
3. ________ courage (remark)
4. ________ accident (avoid)
5. ________ story (believe)
6. ________ jewel (value)
7. ________ weather (change)
8. ________ rule (enforce)
9. ________ effort (laugh)
10. ________ baby (adore)

C Make these words end in **ance** or **ence**.

1. great ________ (perform)
2. teacher's ________ (competent)
3. ________ of wildlife (abundant)
4. grand ________ (enter)
5. big ________ (different)
6. a lot of ________ (patient)
7. great ________ (reluctant)
8. youngster's ________ (dependent)
9. worrying ________ (violent)
10. sweet ________ (fragrant)

D Circle the silent letter in each word.

1. sword 2. castle 3. scheme 4. knuckle 5. lamb

Parent/Teacher Signature Date

Test 1

Choose the correct spelling from the words in the brackets and write it in the space.

1	This dog is both loyal and (fatheful, faithfull, faithful).	1
2	The statue was carved from (marble, marbel, marbell).	2
3	I tried to (conceel, conceil, conceal) the patch in my jeans.	3
4	We ate the (sorsages, sossages, sausages) for lunch.	4
5	You must not (loyta, loiter, loyter) here.	5
6	The ball went over the (boundry, boondary, boundary) line.	6
7	Be careful of that (poisonus, poisinus, poisonous) plant.	7
8	This is a (comfortable, comfortible, cumefortable) chair.	8
9	Be (cereful, carful, careful) when crossing a busy road.	9
10	I used the (sissors, scissors, scissers) to cut the paper.	10
11	Have you made a (deshison, decishin, decision) yet?	11
12	The (athaletics, athletiks, athletics) sports are on tomorrow.	12
13	You need a lot of (preparation, preperation, preparashun).	13
14	That is a difficult (oparation, operation, operashun).	14
15	The children had a (quarrel, quarral, qorril) over the cards.	15

Total correct ______ / 15

Parent/Teacher Signature Date

Test 2

The underlined word in each sentence is spelled incorrectly. Write it correctly in the space.

1	The orchioneer sold the property to the highest bidder.	1
2	The orckestra played many beautiful tunes.	2
3	The plough was connected to the back of the tractar.	3
4	I live in a suberb near Melbourne.	4
5	I wrote out a checkque for twenty dollars.	5
6	There is a kemist shop nearby.	6
7	Lots of mosquitos ruined the picnic.	7
8	The cows stood between us and their calfs.	8
9	There are four different librarys in our city.	9
10	The five dove's nests were in the yard.	10
11	Both of the two lady's dresses are on the bed.	11
12	This supermarket has lots of trollies.	12
13	The table is a sircula shape.	13
14	The couger stalked its prey stealthily.	14
15	Mr Smith is a very jenerous person.	15

Total correct ______ / 15

Parent/Teacher Signature   Date

Test 3

The words in the box have come from Greek, Latin or Old English root words. Match the words to the correct root word below.

autonomy	**wagon**	**transmission**	**metropolitan**	**abbreviate**
bandage	**battle**	**engrave**	**dominate**	**pedestrian**
civilian	**fodder**	**amphibious**	**cosmetics**	**dynamite**

1. mitto (I send) (L)

   ____

2. wegan (to move) (OE)

   ____

3. civis (city) (L)

   ____

4. brevis (short) (L)

   ____

5. bios (life) (G)

   ____

6. gratan (to dig) (OE)

   ____

7. Dominus (Lord) (L)

   ____

8. dunamis (power) (G)

   ____

9. pes, pedis (foot) (L)

   ____

10. beatan (to strike) (OE)

    ____

11. polis (city) (G)

    ____

12. foda (food) (OE)

    ____

13. nomos (law) (G)

    ____

14. bindan (to bind) (OE)

    ____

15. kosmos (beauty) (G)

    ____

Total correct ________
15

Parent/Teacher Signature Date

Useful Words

The following words are frequently misspelled by students of all ages. It is important to consolidate the spelling of these words.

ache
again
always
among
answer
any
been
beginning
believe
blue
break
built
business
busy
buy
can't
choose
colour
coming
cough
could
country
dear
doctor
does
don't
done
early
easy
enough
every
February
forty
friend
grammar
guess
half
having
hear
heard
here
hoarse
hour
instead
just
knew
know
laid
loose
lose
making
many
meant
minute
much
none
often
once
piece
raise
ready
road
said
says
seems
separate
shoes
since
some
straight
sugar
sure
tear
their
there
they
though
through
tired
tonight
too
trouble
truly
Tuesday
two
used
very
wear
Wednesday
week
where
whether
which
whole
women
won't
wood
write
writing
wrote

The following are the words most often misspelled by junior secondary students.

accommodation
acquire
address
adviser
aerial
allowed
altar
aquatic
autumn
believe
beneficial
bicycle
biscuit
broad
business
captain
changeable
circulate
column
coming
commemorate
comparative
cordial
country
county
creature
criticism
customary
deity
delicacy
describe
disappoint
docile
earnest
eighth
eligible
enrol
expel
exquisite
extremely
forehead
foreign
forest
formerly
gardener
gauge
hoping
idle
impostor
independence
iron
journeyed
laid
led
leisure
likelihood
loveliest
magnificent
ministry
movable
movement
naval
noble
northern
nuisance
occur
occurred
oculist
offer
offered
officer
paid
parallel
parliament
persuade
piteous
plentiful
potato
preceding
prefer
preferred
privilege
pursue
quarantine
quarrelled
quarrels
queue
recommend
regretful
regrettable
representative
salmon
scissors
seize
separate
seven
several
significant
similar
skilful
southern
specimen
speech
stooped
stopped
surrender
suspense
their
there
though
thought
through
tidily
travelled
travels
tremor
tried
truly
twelfth
until
violet
weird
wield
yacht
yield

Acronyms

These are pronounceable words made by combining the initial letters or syllables of a string of words. Some are now spelled without capital letters, or with an initial capital only.

AIDS	acquired immune deficiency syndrome
Alcoa	Aluminum Company of America
Anzac	Australian and New Zealand Army Corps
AWOL	absent without leave
CAT	computerised axial tomography
DOS	disk operating system
Fortran	formula translation (programming language)
Interpol	International Criminal Police Organization
laser	light amplification by stimulated emission of radiation
MASH	mobile army surgical hospital
NASA	National Aeronautics and Space Administration
NASCAR	National Association of Sports Car Racing
NATO	North Atlantic Treaty Organization
OPEC	Organization of Petroleum Exporting Countries
Oxfam	Oxford Famine Relief
radar	radio detecting and ranging
RAM	random-access memory
ROM	read-only memory
scuba	self-contained underwater breathing apparatus
SEATO	South-East Asia Treaty Organization
UNESCO	United Nations Education, Social, and Cultural Organization
UNICEF	United Nations International Children's Emergency Fund
UNIVAC	universal automatic computer

Computer language

artificial intelligence
binary number
bit
byte
CPU
cursor
database
disk
disk drive
downtime
floppy disk
hard copy
hard disk
hard drive
hardware
input
interface
joystick
keyboard
language
mainframe computer
modem
mouse
offline
online
output
personal computer (PC)
printout
RAM
ROM
software
spreadsheet
terminal
transistor
video display terminal
word processor

Some Tips for Learning to Spell

Thinking about certain spelling generalisations can help you and, even though some do not work all the time, they can be valuable spelling aids.

- ★ There is only one word that ends in the letters **full** and that is the word **full** itself. All others end in the letters **ful**.
  Examples: wonderful, beautiful, spoonful
- ★ When the letter **i** comes before **gh** it is usually a long sound. Examples: fight, bright, tight
- ★ Every syllable of a word must contain one sounded vowel.
  Example: in/ter/est/ing
- ★ Vowels are more likely to be pronounced short than long.
- ★ If you wish to add a prefix to a word do just that — add it. No spelling changes are necessary.
  Example: **un** + necessary = unnecessary
- ★ The **j** sound is often spelled **dg** or **dge**. Examples: hedging, sludge
- ★ Usually a double consonant or vowel has one sound.
  Example: rabbit, feet
- ★ When two vowels are used together the first usually says its own name.
  Example: gleam, wait
- ★ The final **e** in a one-syllable word is usually silent, as in **hike**. The final **e** makes the vowel say its name. Example: hop, hope
- ★ The **ch** sound is often spelled **tch**. Example: match
- ★ The **k** sound may be made by **c**, **k** or **ck**. Examples: cat, key, rock
- ★ The letters **c** and **g** have both hard and soft sounds.
  Examples: core, city; gold, giant
- ★ The ending **ous** may be used with an **e** or an **i**, depending on the word.
  Examples: extraneous, delicious
- ★ The ending **ance** may be spelled **ence** for some words.
  Examples: entrance, presence
- ★ The ending **tion** may be spelled **cian**, **sian**, **sion**, **tian** for some words.
  Examples: emotion, magician, Persian, explosion, Dalmatian

Self-Assessment Checklist

There are many ways you can improve your spelling performance. Answer the following simple checklist to see if you are following the best practices to improve your spelling.

		Yes	No
★	I keep a record of words that I find difficult to spell and refer to this list when needed.		
★	I use the LOOK, COVER, WRITE, CHECK system to reinforce the spelling of a word so I remember it for future use.		
★	For some tricky or difficult words I purposefully develop spelling memory keys, such as mnemonics, to help me.		
★	I use references (such as dictionaries) to check the spelling of difficult words.		
★	I carefully proofread stories or other written work I have completed.		
★	When I wish to write a word I cannot spell I write the first letter (or first few) letters and then a dash to add it correctly later. (Doing this does not interrupt my train of thought.)		
★	I take an interest in my progress with spelling and I use every opportunity to better my performance.		
★	I am aware of the importance correct spelling is to my future academic and job opportunities.		
★	I take an active and sincere interest in words and study letter patterns and sounds (including syllable stress).		
★	I am aware of word origins and use this to assist my spelling of words derived from the same family or base word.		
★	I am aware that affixes can be added to words to change their part of speech and these additions often cause spelling difficulties.		

Glossary of Terms

adjective
A word that describes nouns or other words.
Examples: **gold** (noun), **golden** (adjective)
wool (noun), **woollen** (adjective)

anagram
A *word* or words that contains exactly the same letters but in a different order.
Examples: **pea**, **ape**; **fowl**, **flow**, **wolf**;
seaside, **disease**

assimilation
Refers to absorbed or assimilated prefixes, when the spelling and sound of the consonant in a prefix has been absorbed into the spelling and sound at the beginning of the *root word* to which the prefix is added. Examples: **ad** + **cumulo** (I make into a heap) = **accumulate;**
come + **ligo** (I join or unite with) = **college**

base word
A *word* to which *prefixes* and *suffixes* can be added. Example: **obey** (base word) + **dis** (prefix) = **disobey** + **ed** (suffix) = **disobeyed**

comparative
An *adjective* that shows a degree of comparison between two or more things.
Examples: **big** (one), **bigger** (two), **biggest** (three or more); Jack is tall but Tom is taller.

complex consonant group
A consonant unit (**ch**, **ck**, **dge**, **tch**) occurring at the end of a *word*, determined by the preceding *vowel* sound. Examples: **tch** follows a short vowel sound, as in **catch**, **fetch**, **itch**, **crutch**;
ch follows a long vowel sound, as in **beach** and **coach**

compound word
A *word* made up of two or more smaller words, often developing first as a hyphenated word.
Example: **butter** + **fly** = **butterfly**.

consonant
A letter in which the air is in some way impeded when pronounced. There are 21 consonants in the alphabet, all the letters that are not *vowels*.

consonant alternation
The process in which the pronunciation of different words derived from the same source changes in the base word. Examples: **sign** to **signal** (silent **g** changes to hard **g**);
music to **musician** (**k** changes to **sh** sound)

consonant blend
When two or more *consonants* come together to blend a sound. Examples: **stick**, **sky**, **brown**, **straw**
Consonant blends may be initial blends (**frog**), medial (middle) blends (**blister**), or final blends (**stamp**).

contraction
A *word* in which one or more letters have been omitted and in their place an apostrophe inserted.
Examples: **I would** becomes **I'd**;
is not becomes **isn't**

digraph
A combination of letters that represents a single sound. There are *consonant* digraphs and *vowel* digraphs. Common consonant digraphs include **sh**, **ch**, **th** and **wh**. (Consonant digraphs at the beginning of a word are called an onset.) A vowel digraph is called a *diphthong*.

diphthong
Two *vowel* sounds that glide together to make a single unit of sound.
Examples: the **oy** in **toy** and the **ou** in **cloud**

eponym
A *word* that has come from the names of a person or place. Example: The word **bantam**, meaning a small foul, comes from a place in Indonesia called Bantam, in Taro.

etymology
The study of the origin and historical development of words.

homograph
A *word* that is spelled the same as another word, but each word is pronounced differently and has a different meaning (a type of *homonym*).
Examples: **desert** (dry barren area) and **desert** (abandon); **close** (near) and **close** (shut)

homonym
A *word* that is spelled and/or pronounced the same as another word but each word has a different meaning. *Homographs* and *homophones* are both types of homonym, and some homonyms are both homographs and homophones.
Examples: **tear** (rip) and **tear** (result of crying);
fair (blond) and **fare** (cost of a train ticket);
bank (place to exchange money) and **bank** (either side of a river)

homophone
A *word* that is pronounced the same as another word, but each word has a different spelling and a different meaning (a type of *homonym*).
Examples: **bear** (a furry animal) and **bare** (naked);
sure (certain) and **shore** (coastline)

letter pattern
A letter sequence that functions as a unit and is related to a consistent category of sound.
Example: **one** = **bone**, **cone**, **tone**

long vowel
The sound of a *vowel* (**a**, **e**, **i**, **o**, **u**) that says its letter name, or is an *r-influenced vowel.*
Examples: **same**, **bacon**, **far**, **concrete**, **fever**, **fine**, **rival**, **fir**, **cone**, **robot**, **core**, **cute**, **student**, **purr**

noun
A *word* that refers to the names of everything around us.

phonics
The systematic relationship between letters and sounds.

phonogram
One of a group of words that end in a common rhyme and that vary only in the beginning *consonant.*
Examples: **back**, **hack**, **lack**, **sack**, **tack**

plural
More than one. Most words make their plurals by adding an **s**. However, there are other ways to make the plurals of words.
Examples: **girl**, **girls**; **watch**, **watches**; **city**, **cities**; **piano**, **pianos**; **knife**, **knives**; **tooth**, **teeth**; **mouse**, **mice**

portmanteau word
A word created by joining a part of one word to a part of another. They were first created by Lewis Carroll, who wrote Alice in Wonderland.
Examples: **brunch** from breakfast and lunch; **smog** from smoke and fog

possessive
A *word* form that shows ownership or possession by adding an apostrophe before an **s** (**'s**) to singular nouns and adding an apostrophe after the *plural* ending for plural nouns.
Examples: one boy**'s** bike, three boys**'** bikes (but five child**ren's** toys).

proper adjective
An adjective formed from a proper noun.
Example: **England** (noun), **English** (adjective); **China** (noun) **Chinese** (adjective)

proper noun
A word that refers to a particular person, place or thing. Examples: **Paul**, **Canada**, **Murray River**

r-influenced vowel
A *vowel* sound that is determined by the letter **r** following it. Example: The **a** in **far** is a *long vowel* sound but the **a** in **fad** is a short vowel sound.

root word
A *word* or word part that has its origin in Old English, Latin or Greek and that provides the basis of many other words.
Example: **aero** (air) = **aerial**, **aeroplane**, **aerobics**

schwa
A vowel sound that often occurs in an unstressed *syllable.*
Example: the uh sound in the first syllable of the word **above**

shortened word
A *word* that, over the years, has become shortened.
Example: **omnibus** (full version in use fifty or more years ago), **bus** (current usage)

short vowel
The sound of a *vowel* (**a**, **e**, **i**, **o** and **u**) that is clipped — a short sound. It is sometimes said short vowel sounds are the "baby" sounds.
Examples: **bat**, **bet**, **bit**, **bottle**, **but**

silent (unsounded) letter
A letter in some words that is not pronounced but is still included in the word. Examples: **lamb**, **know**, **pneumonia**, **sword**, **wrap**

suffix
A *word* ending that alters the word's part of speech (noun to adjective, for example) or meaning. Spelling changes are often needed.
Example: **beauty** + **ful** = **beautiful**

syllable
A sound unit that includes only one sounded vowel. The vowel may be preceded or followed by several consonants. Words can be divided into their syllables. This is a useful spelling technique.
Example: **development** = **de** / **vel** / **op** / **ment**

tense
A word form that shows when an event is happening. Words that change from present to past or future tense often change their spelling in some way. Sometimes the word itself changes or a helping verb is added.
Examples: Today I **play** (present). Yesterday I **played** (past). Tomorrow I will **play** (future).
Today I **freeze** (present). Yesterday I **froze** (past).
Next week I will be **freezing** (future).

vowel
A letter in which the air passes through the mouth without obstruction when pronounced. The letters **a**, **e**, **i**, **o** and **u** are vowels. Note: **y** does the work of the vowels **i** and **e** in words such as **cry** (long **i**), **mystery** (short **i**) and **weary** (long **e**).

vowel alternation
The process by which the pronunciation of a *vowel* changes in the base word while the spelling does not change. Example: the long-to-short vowel change in the related words **crime** and **criminal**

word
A unit of meaning. A word may be a simple *syllable* or a combination of syllables. A word may contain smaller units of meaning within it.

Answers, Class 7

Unit 1
1. entertain
2. vain
3. slain
4. waive
5. explain
6. frail
7. quail
8. maintain
9. failure
10. acquaint
11. available
12. complaint
13. quaint
14. container
15. rainbow
16. faithful

Unit 2
1. guard
2. harp
3. snarl
4. apartment
5. cardigan
6. marvelous
7. harvest
8. charcoal
9. bargain
10. cargo
11. barter
12. departure
13. carnival
14. marble
15. barge
16. particle

Unit 3
A
Long e sound: feast, eagle, crease, grease
Short e sound: sweat, death, thread
Long a sound: break, steak
B
1. measles
2. weapon
3. peach
4. bleach
5. thread
6. breakfast
7. conceal
8. season
9. pleasant
10. steak
11. dread
12. wealth

Unit 4
A
1. exhaust
2. launder
3. saucer
4. tarpaulin
5. sausage
6. nausea
7. gauze
8. authentic
9. audition
10. cauliflower

B
1. moisture
2. loiter
3. asteroid
4. turquoise
5. avoid
6. poisonous
7. poise
8. rejoice
9. voice
10. appointment

Unit 5
A
1. moose
2. bamboo
3. cartoon
4. wooden
5. nook
6. cooking
7. schooner
8. lagoon
9. cockatoo
10. hooded
11. rooster
12. cocoon

B
1. roast
2. loan
3. coast
4. throat
5. approach
6. toadstool
7. loaves
8. cocoa
9. cloak
10. toast

Unit 6
A
1. founder
2. trousers
3. council
4. bounty
5. doubtful
6. voucher
7. scoundrel
8. fountain
9. flounder
10. boundary

B
1. touched
2. moustache
3. cousin
4. youngster
5. double
6. toucan
7. crouton
8. cougar
9. acoustics
10. coupon

Unit 7 Revision
A
1. autumn
2. peach
3. faithful
4. nausea
5. conceal
6. moisture
7. cigar
8. entertain
9. asteroid
10. eagle
11. aide
12. cardigan
13. sausage
14. marble
15. measles
16. poise

B
Short u sound: cousin, couple, double, southern, trouble, touch
Long oo sound: coupon, youth, routine, acoustics, cougar, toucan
C
Long e sound: bleach, cheat, leave, preach, squeak, streak
Short e sound: death, dread, jealous, sweat, thread, heavy

Unit 8 Test 1
1. pleasant
2. available
3. maintain
4. acquaint
5. marble
6. departure
7. bargain
8. breakfast
9. poisonous
10. entertain
11. grease
12. seized
13. saucer
14. bamboo
15. moustache

Unit 9 Test 2
1. doubtful
2. voucher
3. cougar
4. boundary
5. cocoon
6. roast
7. cockatoo
8. cauliflowers
9. poisonous
10. sausages
11. weapon
12. separate
13. carnival
14. faithful
15. marvellous

Unit 10
1. discovery
2. description
3. deceit or deception
4. creation
5. allowance
6. acceptance
7. assistance
8. calculation
9. accusation
10. choice
11. compensation
12. completion
13. departure
14. explosion
15. expectation
16. destruction

Unit 11

1. cautious
2. circular
3. industrious
4. expensive
5. comfortable
6. disastrous
7. humorous
8. injurious
9. fortunate
10. fabulous
11. luxurious
12. influential
13. poisonous
14. woollen
15. victorious
16. triangular

Unit 12

1. tobacco
2. cappuccino
3. successful
4. occurred
5. dessicated
6. traffic
7. forgotten
8. jewellery
9. corrosion
10. accordion
11. broccoli
12. moccasins
13. hiccups
14. accountant
15. affection
16. caffeine

Unit 13

A

1. truly
2. fatally
3. luckily
4. gently
5. easily
6. sweetly
7. lazily
8. suddenly
9. annually
10. anxiously
11. hungrily
12. probably

B

1. merrily
2. patiently

Unit 14 Revision

A

1. cowardly
2. expensive
3. famous
4. woollen
5. starry
6. noisy
7. comfortable
8. favourite
9. faithful
10. beautiful
11. affectionate
12. watery

B

1. billabong
2. ballerina
3. embezzle
4. essential
5. horrible
6. jettison
7. mammoth
8. quarrel
9. scissors
10. village
11. ferret
12. accomplished

C

1. cheaply
2. wearily
3. fatally
4. equally
5. carefully
6. hopefully
7. happily
8. sensibly
9. comfortably
10. anxiously
11. merrily
12. noisily

Unit 15 Test

1. departure
2. accusation
3. assistance
4. influential
5. expensive
6. triangular
7. moccasins
8. occurred
9. antenna
10. annually
11. possibly
12. gently
13. successful
14. comfortable
15. explanation

Unit 16

1. flame
2. athlete
3. please
4. decide
5. assume
6. produce
7. volcano
8. humane
9. cave
10. revise
11. ignite
12. wise
13. divide
14. grave
15. nature
16. episode

Unit 17

1. majority
2. nativity
3. preparation
4. relation
5. competition
6. combination
7. definition
8. division
9. ability
10. invitation
11. resident
12. composition
13. custody
14. stability
15. position
16. recital

Unit 18

1. altitude
2. manual
3. emergency
4. missile
5. operation
6. pedestrian
7. primary
8. property
9. anniversary
10. brief
11. corpse
12. current
13. audience
14. captain
15. civilian
16. dux

Unit 19

A

1. ceiling
2. either
3. seize
4. receipt
5. neither
6. deceived
7. conceited
8. neighbour
9. sleigh
10. vein
11. weight
12. freight

B

1. relieved
2. believe
3. pierced
4. thieves
5. achievement
6. handkerchief
7. applied
8. replied
9. relied
10. shield

Unit 20

1. sneeze
2. teenager
3. canteen
4. auctioneer
5. coffee
6. exceed
7. cheerful
8. breeze
9. corroboree
10. succeed
11. guarantee
12. steeple
13. eerie
14. committee
15. squeeze
16. volunteer

Unit 21

A

1. camera
2. desert
3. passenger
4. mystery
5. verse
6. lantern
7. answer
8. poverty
9. weather
10. liberty
11. battery

12. permanent
13. stationery
14. boomerang
15. northern
16. feather

B

1. certain
2. leather
3. rhinoceros
4. dessert
5. nursery
6. interrupt
7. altered
8. modern
9. machinery
10. persuade

Unit 22

A

1. gorilla
2. organise
3. orchestra
4. portrait
5. tortoise
6. enormous
7. mirror
8. dormitory
9. gorgeous
10. shortage

B

1. author
2. mirror
3. orphan
4. orchard
5. cord
6. portion
7. encore
8. tractor
9. anchor
10. torment

Unit 23

A

1. turnip
2. turkey
3. burger
4. purple
5. burden
6. surgeon
7. suburb
8. purpose
9. turtle
10. blurry

B

ow, as in cow: drowsy, powder, coward, township, trowel

ow, as in know: blown, known, furrow, rainbow, burrow, low

Unit 24

1. parachute
2. anchor
3. chef
4. champion
5. chlorine
6. chemist
7. cheque
8. chapel
9. charity
10. champagne
11. chasm
12. orchestra
13. chassis
14. machine
15. chemical
16. quiche

Unit 25

A

ch sound: charcoal, chilblain, charity, chocolate

k sound: chemist, cholera, chronic, chlorine

sh sound: chassis, champagne, machine, charade

B

1. breeze
2. passenger
3. gorilla
4. auctioneer
5. author
6. camera
7. sneeze
8. portrait
9. liberty
10. steeple
11. enormous
12. answer

C

Long e sound: conceit, deceive, receipt, seize Long a sound: weight, eighty, reign, neighbour

Unit 26 Test 1

1. receipt
2. handkerchief
3. ceiling
4. squeeze
5. succeed
6. guarantee
7. feather
8. interrupt
9. orchestra
10. portrait
11. suburb
12. hamburger
13. cheque
14. chemicals
15. chassis

Unit 27 Test 2

1. chemist
2. anchor
3. purpose
4. dormitory
5. tortoise
6. mirror
7. author
8. poverty
9. eerie
10. auctioneer
11. conceited
12. neighbour
13. vein
14. achievement
15. committee

Unit 28

A

1. crashes
2. brushes
3. dresses
4. buses
5. stitches
6. boxes
7. witches
8. crutches
9. guesses
10. gases
11. foxes
12. garages
13. bullets
14. dishes
15. nieces

B

1. eggs
2. gashes
3. matches
4. peaches
5. bananas
6. arches
7. beaches
8. classes

Unit 29

A

1. monkeys
2. lollies
3. diaries
4. skies
5. armies
6. flies
7. trolleys
8. kidneys
9. storeys
10. libraries
11. fairies
12. duties
13. alleys
14. journeys
15. ponies

B

1. poppies
2. trays,
3. navies
4. ladies
5. bodies,
6. lorries
7. laundries
8. cities
9. donkeys
10. injuries

Unit 30

A

1. reefs
2. scarves
3. knives
4. shelves
5. wolves
6. volcanoes
7. potatoes
8. photos
9. echoes
10. mosquitoes
11. pianos
12. buffaloes
13. loaves
14. calves
15. roofs

B

1. leaves
2. thieves
3. wives
4. carafes
5. giraffes
6. radios
7. potatoes
8. tornadoes

Unit 31

A

1. girl's book
2. tigers' stripes
3. fairy's wings
4. child's toys
5. children's toys
6. dove's nest

B

1. babies'
2. eagle's
3. donkeys'
4. window's
5. foxes'
6. sailors'
7. student's
8. wolves'
9. cousin's
10. lions'
11. daughter-in-law's
12. city's
13. teacher's
14. dog's
15. tables'
16. men's

Unit 32 Revision

1. birds
2. guesses
3. beaches
4. garages
5. brushes
6. donkeys
7. trolleys
8. foxes
9. flies
10. alleys
11. poppies
12. knives
13. potatoes
14. calves
15. pianos
16. thieves

Unit 33 Test

1. tomatoes
2. reefs
3. mosquitoes
4. babies
5. dishes
6. diaries
7. journeys
8. monkeys
9. cities
10. blowflies
11. injuries
12. crutches
13. mirrors
14. boxes
15. photos

Unit 34

1. signwriter
2. oatmeal
3. eardrum
4. cheeseburger
5. earring
6. daybreak
7. skateboard
8. hayfever
9. wallpaper
10. underwear
11. courthouse
12. towtruck
13. overcoat
14. sunglasses
15. lipstick
16. homesick

Unit 35

1. a. pleasure
   b. please
   c. pleasant
2. a. equal
   b. equality
   c. equalled
3. a. encourage
   b. courageous
   c. courage
4. a. lovable
   b. loving
   c. love
5. a. circle
   b. circular
   c. circulation
6. a. fooling
   b. foolish
   c. fool

Unit 36

1. epidemic
2. electricity
3. grammar
4. empathy
5. photograph
6. perimeter
7. cosmetic
8. astronomy
9. optician
10. autograph
11. biography
12. catalogue
13. monopoly
14. democratic
15. metropolis
16. stethoscope

Unit 37

1. battery
2. securely
3. guilty
4. poultry
5. library
6. primary
7. slippery
8. laundry
9. mystery
10. happy
11. luckily
12. quality
13. nursery
14. finally
15. boundary
16. industry

Unit 38

A

1. mirror
2. saucer
3. cursor
4. pitcher
5. molar
6. burglar
7. meteor
8. razor
9. cheddar
10. crater
11. blender
12. cougar
13. tractor
14. lunar
15. powder
16. cancer

B

1. propeller
2. foreigner
3. refrigerator
4. revolver
5. anchor
6. slaughter
7. particular
8. barometer
9. transistor
10. teller
11. circular
12. author

Unit 39

1. alphabet
2. pharmacy
3. hyphen
4. aphids
5. dolphin
6. physician
7. pheasant
8. phobia
9. elephant
10. trophy
11. cipher
12. nephew
13. sphere
14. telephone
15. photocopy
16. pharaoh

Unit 40

A

1. quintet
2. quince
3. quiver
4. quadrangle
5. quartz
6. queue
7. quantity
8. quaver
9. quagmire
10. quotient

B

1. cough ✓
2. bough ×
3. tough ✓
4. neigh ×
5. rough ✓
6. laugh ✓
7. thigh ×
8. through ×

Unit 41

A

1. cuckoo
2. canvas
3. carnivorous
4. cucumber
5. command
6. continents
7. carpet
8. curtains
9. catalogue
10. confectionery

B

1. cereal
2. cyclone
3. circle
4. cider
5. census
6. certain
7. cellar
8. celery

Unit 42

Hard g

1. guitar
2. glacier
3. garbage
4. gorilla
5. gadget
6. galaxy
7. gladiator
8. guilty

Soft g

1. geometry
2. genuine
3. genius
4. gymnasium
5. generous
6. germinate
7. generator
8. geology

Unit 43 Revision

A

Hard g: gallop, gossip, gallery, gallant

Soft g: gesture, ginger, gypsy, genie

Hard c: comet, coffee, control, coconut

Soft c: centipede, cemetery, circus, circuit

B

1. molar
2. plumber
3. editor
4. circular
5. visitor
6. saucer
7. burglar
8. freezer
9. tutor
10. litter
11. donor
12. scholar

C

1. quartz
2. dolphin
3. neigh
4. bequest
5. plough
6. alphabet
7. phobia
8. quadrangle
9. sleigh
10. graph
11. trough
12. quarrel

Unit 44 Test 1

1. guilty
2. primary
3. cursor
4. tractor
5. molar
6. trophy
7. alphabet
8. quantity
9. quartz
10. tough
11. confectionery
12. census
13. genuine
14. phobia
15. circuit

Unit 45 Test 2

1. poultry
2. oxygen
3. mirror
4. cougar
5. anchor
6. powder
7. hyphen
8. pharmacy
9. taught
10. quintet
11. cereal
12. gorilla
13. germinate
14. certain
15. laugh

Unit 46

1. subtraction
2. deletion
3. digestion
4. collision
5. erosion
6. completion
7. explosion
8. division
9. procession
10. infection
11. narration
12. invention
13. revision
14. invasion
15. suggestion
16. persuasion

Unit 47

1. laughable
2. punishable
3. valuable
4. noticeable
5. desirable
6. comfortable
7. affordable
8. changeable
9. believable
10. conceivable
11. preferable
12. avoidable
13. debatable
14. enforceable
15. lovable
16. remarkable

Unit 48

1. effigy
2. surrender
3. supplement
4. attention
5. accomplish
6. aggravate
7. apprehend
8. assemble
9. arrogant
10. succumbed
11. appetite
12. committee
13. accelerate
14. allowance
15. acceptable
16. approximately

Unit 49

1. exposure
2. manicure
3. procedure
4. insecure
5. closure
6. brochure
7. pressure
8. assure
9. endure
10. failure
11. obscure
12. leisure
13. pleasure
14. treasure
15. enclosure
16. composure

Unit 50 Revision

A

1. invention
2. explosion
3. impression
4. injection
5. action
6. conclusion
7. objection
8. production
9. distraction
10. confession
11. erosion
12. imitation

B

1. affordable
2. predictable
3. identifiable
4. adorable
5. admirable
6. manageable
7. noticeable
8. profitable
9. dependable
10. changeable
11. excitable
12. valuable

C

1. enclosure
2. manicure
3. treasure
4. obscure
5. pressure
6. adventure
7. procedure
8. brochure
9. failure
10. mature

Unit 51 Test

1. discussion
2. suggestion
3. valuable
4. enforceable
5. remarkable
6. accomplish
7. effigy
8. insecure
9. pressure
10. irresponsible
11. excitable
12. profitable
13. impression
14. illegal
15. pleasure

Unit 52

A

1. assistant
2. attitude
3. visionary
4. necessary
5. cigarette
6. flexible
7. amiable

8. humane
9. gigantic
10. fugitive
11. canine
12. dormitory
13. molecule
14. fragile
15. retirement
16. bakery

B

1. absentee
2. justice
3. renovate
4. interior
5. royal
6. violent

Unit 53

A

1. autograph
2. misplaced
3. antidote
4. invisible
5. export
6. bicycle
7. extraterrestrial
8. discourage

B

1. circumnavigate
2. dislocate
3. benefactor
4. bicycle
5. benefit
6. explode
7. extraterrestrial
8. non-smoking
9. biscuit
10. disable
11. dispose or expose
12. nonsense
13. deduce
14. disperse
15. expel
16. extraordinary

Unit 54

A

1. p
2. m
3. b
4. g
5. h
6. c
7. n
8. d
9. l
10. j
11. o
12. e
13. i
14. k
15. f
16. a

B

1. d
2. e
3. c
4. b
5. f
6. a

Unit 55

A

1. beach
2. crouch
3. orchard
4. birch
5. brooch
6. couch
7. attach
8. coach
9. pouch
10. poach

B

1. ketch
2. dispatch
3. hopscotch
4. witch
5. latch
6. butterscotch
7. kitchen
8. britches
9. clutch
10. watch
11. sketch
12. satchel

Unit 56

1. mammal
2. final
3. sandal
4. educational
5. cymbal
6. vandal
7. fatal
8. central
9. fossil
10. missile
11. hostile
12. sterile
13. peril
14. docile
15. mobile
16. nostril

Unit 57

A

1. shovel
2. diesel
3. angel
4. kennel
5. chapel
6. jewel
7. barrel
8. quarrel
9. label

B

1. dribble
2. knuckle
3. chuckle
4. bramble
5. saddle
6. beagle
7. ankle
8. cradle
9. rectangle
10. needle
11. kettle
12. bugle

Unit 58

A

1. carpet
2. hatchet
3. tablet
4. velvet
5. jacket
6. basket
7. faucet
8. cricket
9. hornet
10. trumpet
11. wallet
12. comet

B

1. profit
2. summit
3. credit
4. bandit
5. rabbit
6. orbit
7. hermit

Unit 59

A

1. pavement
2. donate
3. silent
4. cleaner
5. cheetah
6. crayon
7. hopeful
8. spider
9. bugle
10. tulip

B

1. disease
2. reptile
3. decay
4. explode
5. terrain
6. surprise
7. perfume
8. compete
9. utility
10. approach

Unit 60

A

1. rhubarb
2. knife
3. autumn
4. beret
5. choir
6. sword
7. pneumonia
8. scent
9. handsome
10. dinghy
11. knuckle
12. hymn

B

1. doubt
2. ghost
3. thumb
4. castle
5. plumber
6. lamb
7. scissors
8. Wednesday
9. chemical
10. often
11. knife
12. debt

C

1. a
2. o
3. o
4. o
5. a
6. o
7. u
8. a

D

1. w
2. t
3. n
4. c

5. g
6. g
7. k
8. t

Unit 61 Revision

A

1. crystal
2. pencil
3. fertile
4. pedal
5. pupil
6. fragile
7. journal
8. futile
9. peril
10. hostile
11. lentil
12. petal

B

1. morsel
2. rectangle
3. parcel
4. knuckle
5. hovel
6. kennel
7. quarrel
8. mingle
9. miracle
10. crumble
11. pastel
12. compel

C

1. helmet
2. rabbit
3. jacket
4. summit
5. habit
6. target
7. scarlet
8. audit
9. blanket
10. spirit
11. bucket
12. digit

Unit 62 Test 1

1. pouch
2. kitchen
3. orchid
4. fossil
5. educational
6. mammal
7. barrel
8. ankle
9. cradle
10. hatchet
11. rabbit
12. wallet
13. juice
14. surprise
15. ballot

Unit 63 Test 2

1. model
2. people
3. magnet
4. trumpet
5. sequel
6. sterile
7. jewel
8. vomit
9. tidal
10. rural
11. council
12. label
13. ample
14. nickel
15. whistle

Unit 64

A

1. defeated
2. prepared
3. repeated
4. whistled
5. perspired
6. drowned
7. skidded
8. travelled
9. dripped
10. stirred
11. begged
12. buried
13. copied
14. denied
15. multiplied
16. occupied

B

1. stopped
2. hurried

Unit 65

A

1. tore
2. became
3. bled
4. drove
5. fell
6. froze
7. struck
8. took
9. spoke
10. sought
11. stole
12. rode
13. sang
14. taught
15. crept
16. fought

B

1. dealt
2. broke
3. began
4. blew
5. ate
6. fled
7. drank
8. was

Unit 66

1. older
2. taller
3. cleverer
4. brighter
5. wiser
6. finer
7. heavier
8. luckier
9. hotter
10. prettier
11. healthier
12. drier
13. bigger
14. happier
15. noisier
16. nastier

Unit 67

1. performance
2. acceptance
3. elegance
4. extravagance
5. fragrance
6. assistance
7. residence
8. violence
9. entrance
10. importance
11. ignorance
12. insurance
13. abundance
14. distance
15. competence
16. difference

Unit 68 Revision

A

1. played
2. wrote
3. cried
4. seek
5. creep
6. froze
7. bleed
8. stole
9. break
10. flee

B

1. prettier
2. wiser
3. noisier
4. fatter
5. hotter
6. wetter
7. luckier

C

1. independence
2. resistance
3. brilliance
4. obedience
5. innocence
6. difference
7. impatience
8. relevance
9. exhuberance
10. evidence

Unit 69 Test

1. buried
2. occurred
3. multiplied
4. stirred
5. drowned
6. sang
7. brighter
8. fatter
9. nastier
10. luckier
11. abundant
12. difference
13. ignorance
14. violence
15. performance

Unit 70

1. morning
2. lesson
3. holy
4. formally
5. bridle
6. moose
7. taught
8. principle
9. bridal
10. formerly
11. lessen
12. taut

13. principal
14. wholly
15. mousse
16. mourning

Unit 71

1 a. in/va/lid b. in/val/id
2 a. pre/sent b. pres/ent
3 a. mi/nute b. min/ute
4 a. re/cord b. rec/ord
5 a. con/vict b. con/vict
6 a. re/fuse b. ref/use

Unit 72

1. nicotine
2. bayonette
3. pasteurisation
4. minute
5. cereal
6. guillotine
7. dandelion
8. port
9. calculator
10. tangerine
11. rugby
12. sandwich

Unit 73 Review

A

Hard c sound: cuckoo, carpet, cucumber, confectionery
Soft c sound: cider, cyclone, celery, circle
Hard g sound: gadget, guitar, guilty, glacier
Soft g sound: genius, genuine, geology, gymnasium

B

1. punishable
2. affordable
3. remarkable
4. avoidable
5. believable
6. valuable
7. changeable
8. enforcable
9. laughable
10. adorable

C

1. performance
2. competence
3. abundance
4. entrance
5. difference
6. patience
7. reluctance
8. dependence
9. violence
10. fragrance

D

1. w
2. t
3. h
4. k
5. b

Unit 74 Test 1

1. faithful
2. marble
3. conceal
4. sausages
5. loiter
6. boundary
7. poisonous
8. comfortable
9. careful
10. scissors
11. decision
12. athletics
13. preparation
14. operation
15. quarrel

Unit 75 Test 2

1. auctioneer
2. orchestra
3. tractor
4. suburb
5. cheque
6. chemist
7. mosquitoes
8. calves
9. libraries
10. doves'
11. ladies'
12. trolleys
13. circular
14. cougar
15. generous

Unit 76 Test 3

1. transmission
2. wagon
3. civilian
4. abbreviate
5. amphibious
6. engrave
7. dominate
8. dynamite
9. pedestrian
10. battle
11. metropolitan
12. fodder
13. autonomy
14. bandage
15. cosmetics